KIDS!
PICTURE YOURSELF
Crocheting

maranGraphics Inc.

Course Technology PTR

A part of Cengage Learning

COURSE TECHNOLOGY
CENGAGE Learning·

Australia • Brazil • Japan • Korea • Mexico • Singapore • Spain • United Kingdom • United States

COURSE TECHNOLOGY
CENGAGE Learning™

Kids! Picture Yourself Crocheting

maranGraphics Inc.

Publisher and General Manager,
Course Technology PTR:
Stacy L. Hiquet

Associate Director of Marketing:
Sarah Panella

Manager of Editorial Services:
Heather Talbot

Marketing Manager: Jordan Casey

Acquisitions Editor: Megan Belanger

Design Consultant: Joanne Yordanou

Development Editor: Sandy Doell

Kid Reviewer: Jennifer Doell

PTR Editorial Services Coordinator:
Judith Littlefield

Interior Layout: Jill Flores

Cover Designer: Mike Tanamachi

Indexer: Katherine Stimson

Proofreader:
Heather Kaufman Urschel

For product information and technology assistance, contact us at
Cengage Learning Customer & Sales Support, 1-800-354-9706

For permission to use material from this text or product, submit all requests online at **cengage.com/permissions**

Further permissions questions can be emailed to
permissionrequest@cengage.com

All trademarks are the property of their respective owners.

Library of Congress Control Number: 2008902394

ISBN-13: 978-1-59863-555-3

ISBN-10: 1-59863-555-7

Course Technology
25 Thomson Place
Boston, MA 02210
USA

Cengage Learning is a leading provider of customized learning solutions office locations around the globe, including Singapore, the United Kingdom, Australia, Mexico, Brazil, and Japan. Locate your local office at: **international.cengage.com/region**

Cengage Learning products are represented in Canada by Nelson Education, Ltd.

For your lifelong learning solutions, visit **courseptr.com**

Visit our corporate website at **cengage.com**

Printed in China
3 4 5 6 7 14 13 12

ABOUT THE AUTHOR

maranGraphics Inc. is a family-run business based in Ontario, Canada.

For over 30 years, the Maran family has produced
friendly and easy-to-use visual learning books.

TABLE OF CONTENTS

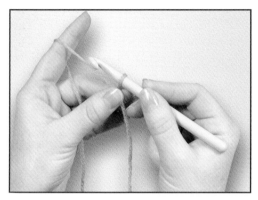

Chapter 3
Learn the Crochet Stitches . . .34

Project 5

Project 6

Part 3

Crocheting is fun and easy to learn. In Part 1 of this book, you'll learn all about the different types of yarn used in crochet. We'll also talk about the crochet hook and give you a look at a few other tools that will help make crocheting easy.

Then we'll go on to learn a few basic stitches, and you'll be on your way to learning a fun new hobby that will keep you entertained and challenged for years.

Supplies and Skills

All you really need to begin crocheting is a ball of yarn, a crochet hook, and some simple instructions. In this chapter, you'll learn how to choose the correct yarn, the right crochet hook for each project, and a few other tools that will help you make your crochet work look quite professional.

Materials and Tools

All About Yarn

Yarn is commonly packaged in balls, skeins, or hanks. Balls are made up of yarn wound into a round shape, while skeins are made up of yarn wound into an oblong shape. It is best to use yarn that has been packaged as a center-pull ball or skein, which means that you can pull the yarn from the center of one end of the ball or skein as you work. This makes the ball or skein less likely to bounce or roll away from you. Balls and skeins are available in various sizes.

Hanks are loosely, but neatly, twisted coils of yarn. Before using a hank, the yarn must be wound into balls. You can have the yarn wound into balls at the store where you purchase the yarn or you can wind the yarn yourself.

Spinning and Ply

Yarn is made by spinning fibers together to form a single strand of yarn. Twisting two or more strands together forms what is called *plied yarn*. For example, twisting two strands together forms a two-ply yarn, while twisting three strands together forms a three-ply yarn. Plied yarn is stronger, smoother, and has a more uniform appearance than a single strand of yarn, but it is not necessarily thicker.

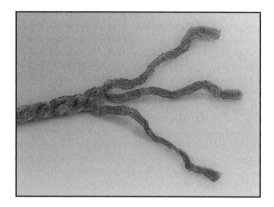

What's It Made of?

The type of fiber that a yarn is made of will impact all kinds of behaviors of that yarn: how stretchy (or elastic) it is, how warm (or insulating) it is, how hard or easy it is to wash, and even how easy or difficult the yarn will be to actually crochet with. Understanding these "behaviors" of different fibers will help you choose which yarn to use for your crocheted projects.

Yarn can be made from natural or synthetic fibers. There are two types of natural fibers: plant fibers and animal fibers. Plant fibers are made from plants, such as cotton and hemp plants. Animal fibers are derived from animals such as sheep and rabbits. Synthetic fibers are produced from chemical sources.

Plant Fibers

Plant fibers are made from cellulose, which is the main component of plant tissue. Plant fibers produce garments that are durable, breathable, and absorb moisture extremely well. Plant fibers are also hypo-allergenic, which makes them an excellent choice for people who are allergic to animal fibers such as wool.

When choosing yarn for a project, you should keep in mind that yarn produced from plant fibers does not provide as much insulation as yarn derived from animal fibers.

Cotton

Cotton is a very absorbent and quick-drying fiber, which makes cotton garments comfortable to wear in hot weather. Since cotton is stronger wet than dry, no special care is required when washing it. This makes cotton an ideal fiber for crocheting items that are frequently washed, such as dish cloths and baby items.

Compared to wool, cotton is a more difficult fiber to work with; it is not as elastic and shows imperfections in your crocheted garments more easily.

The highest-quality and most expensive types of cotton include Egyptian, Sea Island, and Pima. Egyptian cotton is known for its soft, luxurious texture. Sea Island cotton is prized for its silky feel and lustrous appearance. Pima cotton is valued for its strength.

Animal Fibers

Animal fibers are protein-based and come from the coat of animals such as sheep, goats, and rabbits. Animal fibers provide good insulation, which helps keep you warm in cold weather and cool in warm weather. Animal fibers are also soft, lightweight, absorbent, and stretch resistant.

Animal fibers are vulnerable to moth larvae, as the larvae eat the protein-based fiber. They can also create a rougher, more scratchy feeling fabric, so if you're choosing fabric for, say, a baby hat or scarf for a friend, rub the ball of yarn on your face to get an idea of how it will feel in the finished product.

Wool

Wool is spun from fleece that has been sheared from sheep and is the most popular yarn choice for crocheters. Wool is warm, durable, elastic, and resists wrinkling. Wool is also very absorbent, which makes it dye-friendly.

There are several different types of wool available, with each type having its own special properties. For example, Merino wool from the Merino sheep is very fine and soft, while Pure New wool is rougher but is more water resistant due to increased amounts of lanolin.

Wool is often used for crocheting items such as sweaters, hats, mittens, and scarves. Wool garments may not be suitable for people who have allergies or sensitive skin.

Alpaca

Alpaca fiber comes from the coat of a llama-like animal of the same name that lives in South America. Alpaca yarn is soft, silky, light-weight, and very warm. Because the natural color of alpaca ranges from beige to brown, alpaca fibers must be bleached before being dyed another color. Often you can find un-dyed, un-bleached yarn, though, in many beautiful shades of browns and grays. Alpaca is not as expensive as cashmere, but it is more costly than wool. Alpaca is commonly used to crochet sweaters and scarves.

Angora

Angora, which is derived from the fur of the Angora rabbit, is soft, delicate, warm, and downy, but it tends to shed. Angora is expensive, so it is often blended with other fibers to lower the cost and increase the strength of the resulting yarn. Angora is commonly used for crocheting items such as hats and sweaters.

Cashmere

Cashmere, which is made from the hair of the Cashmere goat, is one of the softest and most luxurious yarns available. Like wool, cashmere dyes easily and makes a resilient fabric that resists stretching and wrinkling. Cashmere is very expensive, so it is often blended with wool to create a stronger yarn at a lower price. Cashmere is often used to make sweaters and accessory items, such as scarves.

Silk

Silk yarn is produced from silkworm cocoons that have been unraveled to form long, lustrous fibers. Silk garments have a wonderful drape and feel. Silk is strong, but not very resilient.

As a result, silk garments tend to stretch with wear. Because silk is expensive, it is often blended with other fibers to lower the cost. Due to the special care required to clean silk, crocheters often use silk just for special projects.

Man-Made Fibers

Man-made fibers are derived from chemical sources and are usually inexpensive. Yarn produced from man-made fibers is generally easy to care for, which makes it ideal for crocheting items that are frequently washed, such as blankets, afghans, and sweaters. You should be careful when ironing an item made from man-made fiber, as these types of fibers can lose their shape and even melt if too much heat is applied.

Man-made fibers do not offer the warmth, absorbency, or elasticity of natural fibers. Man-made fibers are often blended with natural fibers to obtain some of these properties and produce a higher quality yarn.

Nylon

Nylon, or polyamide, is the strongest man-made fiber and is often added to other fibers to provide durability and prevent pilling. When blended with other fibers, nylon is useful for crocheting frequently used items, such as mittens. Fabrics made predominantly from nylon do not breathe well and are prone to static cling, but are water resistant.

Acrylic

Yarn made from acrylic is lightweight and strong. Although acrylic lacks insulating properties and tends to pill (*pilling* is the formation of little balls of fiber on the surface of the garment), this fiber remains very popular with crocheters because of its low price, availability, and washability. When blended with wool, acrylic is more enjoyable to work with and wear. Acrylic is used for crocheting sweaters, hats, mittens, afghans, and many other items.

Metallic Fibers

Metallic fibers incorporate small amounts of metal to create yarn that sparkles and glitters. Metallic fibers are not very strong and so they are usually blended with other fibers to increase their strength. Metallic fibers are increasing in popularity and are commonly used to crochet evening wear and holiday items.

Novelty Yarns

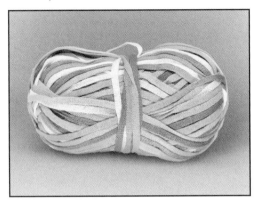

Novelty yarn has an interesting texture and appearance, making it fun to use but often more difficult work with. You can use novelty yarn to crochet many items, including scarves, purses, and cuffs or collars for sweaters. Novelty yarn can be made from natural, man-made, or blended fibers and is often produced by twisting different yarns together or twisting multiple strands of the same yarn together at different tensions. Popular examples of novelty yarn include bouclé, chenille, and eyelash.

Yarn Weights

Yarn is categorized by weight, which is simply the thickness of the yarn. The weight of the yarn you use affects the appearance of the item you crochet as well as how long the project will take to complete. For example, a thicker yarn produces a warmer, bulkier, item, and will likely take less time to complete.

Determining a yarn weight can be confusing because different manufacturers and different countries use their own names for each weight.

Here are some of the most common weights (from thinnest to thickest). For the purposes of illustration, the yarn weights pictured below are displayed in proportion to each other, but are not actual size.

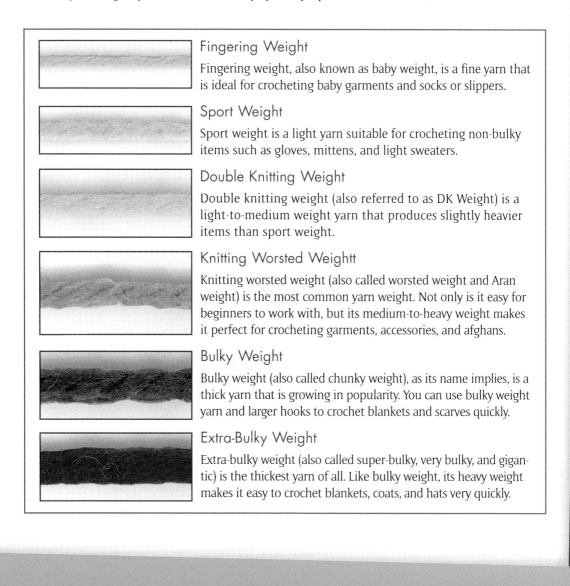

Fingering Weight

Fingering weight, also known as baby weight, is a fine yarn that is ideal for crocheting baby garments and socks or slippers.

Sport Weight

Sport weight is a light yarn suitable for crocheting non-bulky items such as gloves, mittens, and light sweaters.

Double Knitting Weight

Double knitting weight (also referred to as DK Weight) is a light-to-medium weight yarn that produces slightly heavier items than sport weight.

Knitting Worsted Weightt

Knitting worsted weight (also called worsted weight and Aran weight) is the most common yarn weight. Not only is it easy for beginners to work with, but its medium-to-heavy weight makes it perfect for crocheting garments, accessories, and afghans.

Bulky Weight

Bulky weight (also called chunky weight), as its name implies, is a thick yarn that is growing in popularity. You can use bulky weight yarn and larger hooks to crochet blankets and scarves quickly.

Extra-Bulky Weight

Extra-bulky weight (also called super-bulky, very bulky, and gigantic) is the thickest yarn of all. Like bulky weight, its heavy weight makes it easy to crochet blankets, coats, and hats very quickly.

Choosing and Buying Yarn

When buying yarn, there are several things you should consider. First, *you should purchase the best yarn you can afford.* Higher quality yarn is not only nicer to work with, but you will appreciate the look and feel of better quality yarn when your project is complete. You should also make sure the yarn you choose will be comfortable to wear. For example, if you are crocheting a wool scarf, hold the yarn to your neck to see how it feels.

Manufacturers dye yarn in batches called *lots*, with each lot assigned a specific number. Even though they use the same dyes in each lot to achieve a specific color, yarns of the same color but dyed in different lots will not necessarily look the same; there will be subtle (and sometimes not so subtle) variations in the color of the yarn. Always check the dye lot number on each package of yarn you buy for a project to make sure they are all the same. You should also make sure to buy enough of the yarn that you will use for a specific project. It is a sad day when you realize you need one more ball of yarn and you go back to the store to find that they are out of your matching lot number.

Lastly, your pattern may provide instructions for crocheting the project in several different sizes. Before going to the store, decide which size you are going to crochet. The size you choose will determine how much yarn you need to purchase.

Where to Buy Yarn

You can purchase yarn from several types of stores. Craft stores offer middle of the road yarns. Specialty yarn shops and boutiques carry a wider variety of yarns, including high-end, fancy, and novelty yarns. Specialty shops often have experienced staff that can offer advice and help you choose yarn (and may even give you free help and advice if you get stuck on a project if you buy from them). What's more, specialty shops (and even some craft stores, for that matter) offer crochet lessons, as well.

You can even buy yarn on the Internet, such as on eBay or online stores. When shopping on the Internet, you should buy yarn you are familiar with so that you are not disappointed by the texture or color when the yarn arrives.

Substituting Yarn

A pattern will suggest the yarn you should use for your crocheting project, but you can replace the yarn depending on the yarn's cost, availability, or simply your own preference. If you decide to use another yarn, look for a yarn with the same weight, length, and recommended hook size as the suggested yarn. You can also compare the recommended gauge on the package to the one called for in your pattern to get a better idea if it will work. (See Chapter 2, "Crochet Basics," to learn all about gauge.) And when in doubt, ask a salesperson for help.

Remember that choosing a different fiber type or color than the pattern suggests will affect the feel and look of the garment you are knitting.

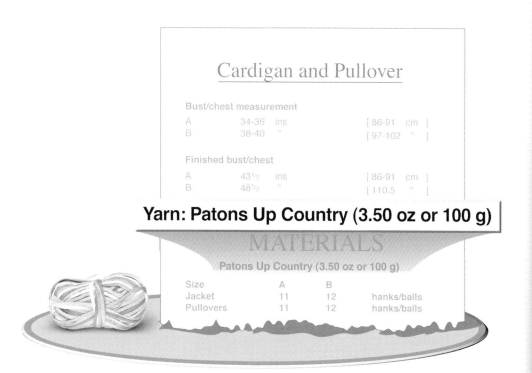

Cardigan and Pullover

Bust/chest measurement

A	34-36	ins	[86-91	cm]
B	38-40	"	[97-102	"]

Finished bust/chest

A	43½	ins	[86-91	cm]
B	48½	"	[110.5	"]

Yarn: Patons Up Country (3.50 oz or 100 g)

MATERIALS

Patons Up Country (3.50 oz or 100 g)

Size	A	B	
Jacket	11	12	hanks/balls
Pullovers	11	12	hanks/balls

How to Read a Yarn Label

When purchasing yarn, you should carefully read the label wrapped around the ball of yarn. The label will tell you all kinds of important information and can help you determine whether the yarn is suitable for your project. You may find the following information on a yarn label.

Manufacturer's Name and Address. The name and address of the yarn manufacturer.

Brand Name. The manufacturer's name for the line of yarn.

Fiber Content. The fiber the yarn is made of, for example, 100% Acrylic.

Ply. The number of strands that have been twisted together to make up the yarn.

Yarn Thickness. The thickness classification of the yarn, also called yarn weight. For example, worsted weight yarn is of medium thickness and is perfect for crocheting clothing and afghans.

Weight. Refers to how much the package of yarn actually weighs. Common weights include 1.75 ounces (50 g) and 3.5 ounces (100 g).

Yarn Length. The total length of the yarn in the ball measured in yards or meters. Some fibers are heavier than others, so focus on yarn length (not weight) to determine how much yarn the ball contains.

Suggested Hook Size and Gauge. The recommended hook size to use with the yarn. (Gauge refers to the number of stitches and rows you should have when you crochet a square of fabric with the suggested hook size.)

Care Instructions. Words or symbols that indicate how to care for the fabric.

Special Processing. The special treatments the yarn has been subjected to, such as Colorfast (prevents colors from fading or running) and Superwash (allows wool to be machine washed and dried without shrinkage).

Color Name and Number. The name and/or number of the yarn color.

Dye Lot Number. The specific lot number of that ball of yarn. When you buy a specific color of yarn, the color may vary slightly between different dye lots. To ensure the color remains consistent in your project, always buy the yarn from the same dye lot number. To prevent running out, it is a good idea to buy a little more than you think you will need.

Caring for Your Crocheted Projects

Your crochet projects take a lot of time and money to create, so you want to make sure that you wash them the right way. Handmade crocheted pieces are more likely to shrink than store-bought garments. To help preserve your crocheted items, pay close attention to the care symbols found on the yarn labels and follow the recommended cleaning instructions carefully. Depending on the type of yarn used, the garment will need to be either washed or dry cleaned. See the following chart for a list of common care symbols.

> Tip ● Tip ● Tip ● Tip ● Tip ● Tip ● Tip ● Tip
>
> It is a good idea to save at least one of the labels from each type of yarn you use, at least for a little while after you complete your project. You'll need the information on the label to know how to best care for your crocheted treasures. In fact, some crocheters like to keep journals about their projects, and they paste the label information in their journal. It is also a great way to remember that awesome yarn you like so much—or that one you never want to use again!
>
> Tip ● Tip ● Tip ● Tip ● Tip ● Tip

When you hand-wash crocheted pieces, use a gentle detergent and never let the garment soak in the water for an extended period of time. You should squeeze the garment to remove dirt and then empty the water from the wash basin. Rinse the item one or two times, carefully removing as much water as possible. After taking the garment out of the wash basin, position it on a colorfast towel and loosely roll up the towel to soak up even more water. You can then reshape the garment to its proper dimensions and let it air dry.

When you use a washing machine to clean crochet work, make sure to use the correct water temperature. To help keep your crocheted garments looking great, you should machine wash each item by itself to avoid pilling. You can also try washing the garment in a pillowcase to keep it from stretching out. To prevent creasing and wrinkling, you should remove the garment from the washing machine as soon as the cycle is finished.

Symbol	Means This	Symbol	Means This
	Do not wash		Tumble dry, no heat
	Hand wash		Tumble dry, low heat
	Machine wash at displayed temperature		Tumble dry, medium heat
	Machine wash, cold water		Tumble dry, high heat
	Machine wash, warm water		Tumble dry, no heat, gentle cycle
	Machine wash, hot water		Tumble dry, low heat, gentle cycle
	Machine wash, cold water, gentle cycle		Tumble dry, medium heat, gentle cycle
	Machine wash, warm water, gentle cycle		Do not press
	Machine wash, hot water, gentle cycle		Do not press with steam
	Do not use chlorine bleach		Press with a cool iron
	Chlorine bleach can be used		Press with a warm iron
	Non-chlorine bleach can be used		Press with a hot iron
	Dry flat		Do not dry clean
	Do not tumble dry		Dry clean

All About Crochet Hooks

You require only two items to crochet—the yarn of your choice and a crochet hook. With these simple tools you can create many beautiful crocheted pieces.

Crochet hooks are available in various materials, including steel, plastic, aluminum, wood, and bamboo. Steel crochet hooks are small and are often used to crochet intricate items, such as lace doilies, with fine yarn or cotton. Larger crochet hooks are usually made from lightweight materials such as plastic or aluminum.

Although most crochet hooks are similar in length (approximately 6 inches) and appearance, the shape of the hook at the end of a crochet hook can vary slightly between manufacturers. For example, some hooks are more rounded while others are pointier. You can experiment with different brands to find the crochet hooks you prefer.

Crochet Hook Sizes

There are three systems commonly used to classify crochet hook sizes—US, metric, and UK. The US system classifies crochet hook sizes using a letter and/or a number.

You will usually select your crochet hook based on the size suggested in your pattern. When choosing a crochet hook, it is important to remember that different manufacturers may label the same crochet hook size differently.

The following chart is a guideline for aluminum and plastic crochet hook sizes. Sizes for steel crochet hooks range from 14US (.70–.75 mm) to 00US (3 mm).

US	Metric	UK
B/1	$2^{1}/4$ mm	12
C/2	$2^{3}/4$ mm	11
D/3	$3^{1}/4$ mm	10
E/4	$3^{1}/2$ mm	9
F/5	$3^{3}/4$ mm	8
G/6	$4^{1}/4$ mm	7
H/8	5 mm	6
I/9	$5^{1}/2$ mm	5
J/10	6 mm	4
K/$10^{1}/2$	$6^{1}/2$ mm	2
L/11	8 mm	
N/15	9 mm	
P	10 mm	
Q	16 mm	
S	19 mm	

Handy Tools and Timesavers

There are several additional items you should have on hand while crocheting. You can find the following inexpensive tools at most craft and knitting stores.

Scissors

Crochet patterns may direct you to "break" yarn, which simply means to cut it. To cut yarn, use small, sharp scissors, preferably ones that you can fold up or put in a case to avoid damaging your project when you put it away.

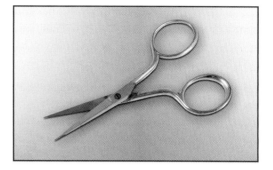

Tape Measure

You use a tape measure to determine the measurements of various parts of your project, such as the sleeve length of a sweater you are crocheting or length of a scarf. (You also will use it to take your own measurements to figure out which size of garment you need to make.) A good tape measure is flexible, but it should not stretch.

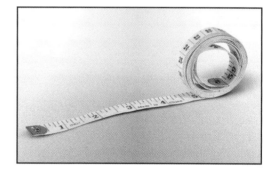

Safety Pins

Safety pins can be used in a variety of situations when crocheting, such as marking the right side of your garment. You can purchase coil-less safety pins, which will not tangle in yarn, from specialty needlework shops.

Project Bag

You should store each of your crochet projects, including a copy of the pattern and the tools you are working with, in a separate canvas or cotton bag. The ideal project bag is large enough to hold everything you need for your current project.

Tapestry Needles

Tapestry needles, also known as sewing, darning, and yarn needles, look like large sewing needles and have a dull tip. These needles are often used to sew pieces of crocheted fabric together and weave in yarn ends. Considering that tapestry needles come in many different sizes, make sure the eye of the needle is large enough for the yarn you are using to pass through.

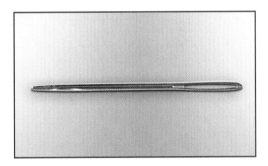

Straight Pins

Straight pins are used to hold crocheted pieces together as you complete your project. The best straight pins have large heads so that you do not lose sight of them in your project. Straight pins are also vital for blocking.

Stitch Markers

Stitch markers are used to leave a visual reminder where pattern changes occur. Stitch markers are available in different colors and can be either a solid or a split ring. Split rings are especially handy because you can insert them in the middle of a row of stitches.

CHAPTER 2

This chapter will introduce you to the fundamental techniques and terms used in crocheting. You will learn how to hold the yarn and crochet hook as well as how to make a foundation chain. This chapter also explains how to read a crochet pattern, so you can quickly get started on your crochet projects.

Crochet Basics

Introduction to Crochet

Crocheting is a fun activity that is easy to learn and requires only a ball of yarn and a crochet hook to practice. You can quickly create a variety of useful crochet projects ranging from decorative items, such as lace doilies, to more functional items, such as scarves, sweaters, or blankets.

Crocheting and Knitting: What's the Difference?

Crocheting and knitting are similar in that they both create fabric by interlacing a series of loops to form stitches. However, there are several differences between the two crafts.

Crocheting is generally faster than knitting and is considered by many to be easier to learn. You use one crochet hook to create stitches instead of the two needles required for knitting. In crochet, only one loop is active at a time, while in knitting, an entire row of stitches is usually active.

Crochet stitches are a different size and shape than stitches created by knitting, so the fabrics produced by each craft differ in appearance and texture. Crocheted fabrics tend to be bulkier and drape less freely than knitted fabrics.

Why Crochet?

There are many reasons you might want to learn to crochet. In today's fast-paced world, crochet is an ideal hobby because it is a creative and satisfying craft that can help you relax. Crocheting has been likened to meditation in the way the repetitive movements of the crochet hook and yarn relieve stress. Another emotional benefit is the pride and pleasure you derive from a completed crochet project that you can use or give as a gift.

Crocheting is convenient for a busy lifestyle; you can complete a project over time, putting it aside and resuming work whenever you like. Crochet is also a portable pastime. You can take your project with you and work on it while riding in the car, when visiting relatives, or just about anywhere you go.

FUN FACT
Crocheting was first practiced by European nuns in the 16th century who used the craft to create fine decorative lace.

Crochet: The New Generation

Although no longer practiced out of the necessity to produce garments and other items for personal use, crochet is still a very popular craft. Today, many people crochet simply for the joy of it. Once the domain of grandmothers, crocheting has, in recent years, become a trendy pastime for people of all ages. Many kids are taking up crocheting as a hobby and pastime.

Crochet and the Internet

The Internet is a valuable resource for new and experienced crochet enthusiasts who want information about crocheting and the opportunity to interact and share ideas with others around the world. The following are some popular web sites devoted to sharing information about crocheting.

FUN FACT
The word crochet means hook in French.

Popular Crochet Web Sites	
Crochet Guild of America	crochet.org
Craft Yarn Council of America	www.craftyarncouncil.com
The National NeedleArts Association	www.tnna.org
YarnStandards.com	www.yarnstandards.com
CrochetAndKnitting.com	www.crochetandknitting.com
Crochet 'N' More	www.crochetnmore.com
The Red Sweater	www.theredsweater.com/tips.html
Needlepointers.com	www.needlepointers.com
Learn to Knit and Crochet	www.learntoknit.com
By The Hook	www.angelfire.com/biz/bythehook

Hold a Crochet Hook

You can hold a crochet hook in one of two ways. Both positions provide good support and allow you to work comfortably and quickly. You can try both positions to determine which one best suits you.

The most popular method is to hold the crochet hook as if you were holding a pencil, using your thumb and index finger to grip the flat area of the crochet hook. Alternatively, you can hold the crochet hook as if you were holding a knife, using your thumb, index finger, and middle finger to hold the flat area of the crochet hook. Your free hand is used to hold the yarn.

If you are left-handed, you can hold a crochet hook in your left hand using either of the positions discussed here. Since this book is written for right-handed people, if you are left-handed, substitute right for left and left for right throughout the steps in this book.

Position 1

1 Hold the crochet hook in your right hand as if you were holding a pencil. Your thumb and index finger hold the flat section of the crochet hook.

Position 2

1 Hold the crochet hook in your right hand as if you were holding a knife. Your thumb, index finger, and middle finger hold the flat section of the crochet hook. Your other fingers can help support the crochet hook.

Make a Slip Knot

To begin crocheting, you must first make a slip knot to secure the yarn to the crochet hook.

When you make a slip knot, you create a loop with your yarn, leaving a "tail" that measures about 6 inches between the loop and the end of the yarn. You then use the crochet hook to pull the strand of yarn connected to the ball through the loop.

The final step is pulling the two yarn ends away from each other to tighten the slip knot around the crochet hook.

For more information on chain stitches, see the "Make a Chain" section.

1 Make a loop with your yarn, allowing the strand of yarn connected to the ball to hang down behind the loop.

2 Insert the crochet hook through the loop, from front to back.

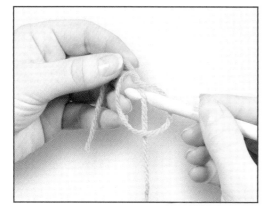

3 Catch the strand of yarn hanging behind the loop with the crochet hook and pull the yarn through the loop.

4 Gently pull both ends of the yarn in opposite directions to tighten the slip knot around the crochet hook.

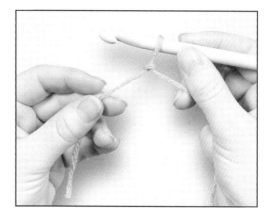

5 Slide the slip knot up the crochet hook until the slip knot is 1 or 2 inches from the hook.

You are now ready to begin crocheting.

Hold the Yarn

1 Hold the crochet hook in your right hand.

2 With the yarn in your left hand, place the yarn between your pinky and ring fingers. Then wrap the yarn counterclockwise around your pinky finger.

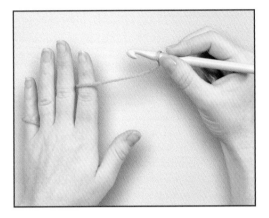

3 Weave the yarn under your ring and middle fingers and then over your index finger.

4 To start crocheting, grasp the slip knot on the crochet hook using the thumb and middle finger of your left hand.

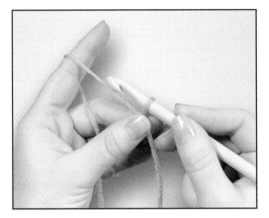

Use your pinky, ring, and middle fingers to hold the yarn loosely in your left hand.

You can lift and lower your left index finger to control the tension of the yarn.

Make a Foundation Chain

To start your crochet project, you need to make chain stitches, which are often called *chains*. The first row of chain stitches you complete is called the *foundation chain* and will form the bottom edge of your crochet project. You will crochet all the other rows in your project on top of the foundation chain.

A *yarn over* is the basic movement used to create chain stitches and every other crochet stitch. A yarn over involves bringing the yarn over the crochet hook and catching the yarn with the hook. In instructions, the yarn over is represented by the abbreviation **yo**.

Chain stitches are not only created for the foundation chain. You can create chain stitches at any location in your project. You should work your chain stitches at the thickest part of the crochet hook, usually 1 or 2 inches from the hook. This will help ensure your chain stitches are not too tight. In patterns, the chain stitch is represented by the abbreviation **ch**. For example, **ch12** indicates that you should make 12 chain stitches.

1 Make a slip knot on the crochet hook.

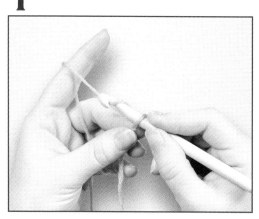

2 Hold the crochet hook in your right hand, with the yarn wrapped around the fingers of your left hand.

3 Bring the yarn over the crochet hook from back to front.

4 Catch the yarn with the crochet hook.

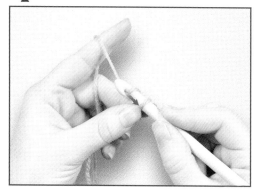

5 Slide the hook and the strand of yarn through the loop on the crochet hook, allowing the loop to fall off the crochet hook.

> Bringing the yarn over the crochet hook and catching the yarn with the hook is known as a yarn over (**yo**).

You have created one chain stitch.

A loop remains on the crochet hook.

6 Slide the loop down the crochet hook until the loop is 1 or 2 inches from the hook.

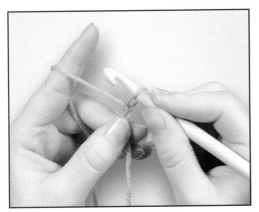

7 Repeat steps 3 to 6 for each chain stitch you want the foundation chain to contain.

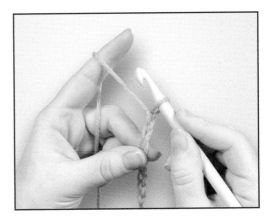

As you make new chain stitches, move your left thumb and middle finger up the foundation chain to hold your work.

Tip • Tip • Tip • Tip • Tip • Tip • Tip • Tip

The foundation chain will become the bottom edge of your work.

Tip • Tip • Tip • Tip • Tip • Tip • Tip • Tip

Counting chain stitches is an essential part of any crochet project. To count the chain stitches in your foundation chain, make sure the front of the foundation chain is facing you. The front of the foundation chain displays a row of Vs and is flat. The back of the foundation chain is bumpy. Starting with the last chain stitch you completed, count every chain stitch in the foundation chain. Do not count the loop on the crochet hook as a chain stitch or the slip knot you made to secure the yarn to the crochet hook.

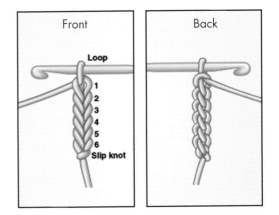

Read a Crochet Pattern

Crochet patterns provide you with all the information you need to create a crocheted project, including detailed instructions that use abbreviations, symbols, and terms. With practice, you will be able to read crochet pattern instructions quickly and easily. Before beginning a project, you should read all the instructions included in the pattern so that you have a good understanding of how the entire project will be made.

Size

A crochet pattern usually specifies the approximate dimensions of the finished project. When a project can be made in multiple sizes, the pattern specifies the additional sizes in parentheses, such as "Small (Medium, Large)." Throughout the pattern, you will find the instructions for the additional sizes in parentheses. For example, a pattern may specify "ch 30 (32, 34)," which means you should crochet 30 chain stitches for the small size, 32 chain stitches for the medium size, or 34 chain stitches for the large size.

Materials

A pattern will tell you the type, color, weight, and amount of the yarn you will need. A pattern will also indicate the crochet hook size you should use and include information about any additional materials you will need, such as buttons.

Gauge

A pattern indicates the gauge, or *tension*, required to ensure that your finished project will be the correct size. Gauge is the number of stitches and rows you should have in a sample piece of crocheted fabric when you use the same crochet hook and yarn you will use for the project.

Abbreviations

Pattern instructions are written using abbreviations. A list of abbreviations used in the pattern you are following may be included in the pattern. The following is a list of some commonly used crochet abbreviations. For a more extensive list, see the appendix at the end of this book.

ch(s)	chain(s)
dc	double crochet
hdc	half double crochet
sc	single crochet
sl st	slip stitch
st(s)	stitch(es)
tr	triple crochet

Symbols

Here are some commonly used symbols you will find in crochet patterns.

*

An asterisk (*) marks the beginning of a set of instructions that you will repeat. You work the instructions following the asterisk once and then repeat the instructions the specified number of times. For example, a pattern may specify "*sc in next 2 sts, ch 2, rep from * 4 times," which means you work the instructions following the first asterisk a total of five times.

FUN FACT
Crochet isn't just for afghans! With the right yarn and hook, you can crochet everything from beautiful jewelry to durable rugs, potholders, and purses.

** **

Double asterisks (**) mark a long section of instructions that you will be asked to repeat later in the pattern. For example, if a section of the front of a sweater is worked the same as the back of a sweater, the instructions for the back are enclosed in double asterisks. The instructions for the front may state "Work from ** to ** as given for Back."

( ) or [ ]

You work the instructions enclosed in brackets as many times as indicated by the number immediately following the brackets. For example, if a pattern states "(3 dc in next ch st. Ch 1) 3 times," you work the instructions enclosed in the brackets three times. Brackets can also indicate that you should work all the instructions into one stitch. For example, if a pattern states "(hdc, ch 2, hdc) in the next st," you work all the instructions enclosed in the brackets into the next stitch.

Terms

Here are some commonly used terms you will find in crochet patterns.

Back loop: Of the two top horizontal strands of a stitch, the strand that is farthest away from you.

Front loop: Of the two top horizontal strands of a stitch, the strand that is closest to you.

Post: The vertical part of a stitch. Also called a leg or bar.

Work even or Work straight: Work in the established pattern without increasing or decreasing stitches.

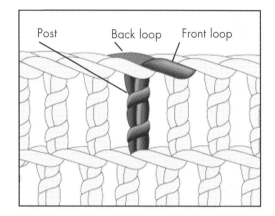

FUN FACT

When you put together your crocheting toolkit, a good place to look before going to the store is your grandma's or aunt's house. Lots of times they will have yarn and crochet hooks around, even if you've never seen them crochet. Ask to see the sewing kits of other family members.

CHAPTER 7

Once you are comfortable with the fundamentals of crocheting, you are ready to work with crochet stitches. In this chapter you will learn how to make the basic crochet stitches, including single, half double, double, and triple crochet stitches. You will also learn how to shape your work by increasing and decreasing stitches and how to crochet in rounds, as well as techniques for finishing your work.

Learn the Crochet Stitches

Single Crochet

Row 1

The single crochet stitch is a short stitch that creates a tightly woven fabric. In patterns, the single crochet stitch is abbreviated as **sc**. A row may be made up entirely of single crochet stitches or a combination of different stitches.

To work a row of single crochet stitches into the foundation chain, you work the first single crochet stitch into the second chain stitch. Skipping the first chain stitch allows the row of single crochet stitches to stand at its proper height.

When locating the second chain stitch, make sure the front of the foundation chain is facing you. The front of the foundation chain displays a row of Vs. Also, make sure you do not count the loop on the crochet hook as a chain stitch.

Since you skip the first chain stitch, the number of single crochet stitches in the completed row will be one less than the number of chain stitches in the foundation chain. For example, if you have 10 chain stitches in the foundation chain, you will have nine single crochet stitches in the finished row.

1 Make a foundation chain to start your crochet project. To make a foundation chain, see Chapter 2.

2 Locate the second chain stitch from the crochet hook.

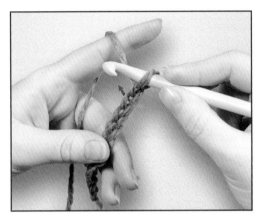

3 Insert the crochet hook under the top loop of the chain stitch from front to back.

4 Bring the yarn over the crochet hook from back to front.

5 Catch the yarn with the hook of the crochet hook.

6 Slide the hook and the strand of yarn through the first loop on the crochet hook, allowing the loop to fall off the crochet hook.

Tip • Tip • Tip • Tip • Tip • Tip • Tip • Tip

If the loop slips off the crochet hook while you are crocheting, first make sure the front of your work is facing you. Then insert the crochet hook through the front of the loop. Before inserting the crochet hook through the loop, make sure the loop is not twisted.

Tip • Tip • Tip • Tip • Tip • Tip • Tip • Tip

❊ You now have two loops on the crochet hook.

7 Bring the yarn over the crochet hook from back to front.

8 Catch the yarn with the hook of the crochet hook.

9 Slide the hook and the strand of yarn through the two loops on the crochet hook, allowing the two loops to fall off the crochet hook.

❊ You now have one loop on the crochet hook.

❊ You have created one single crochet stitch.

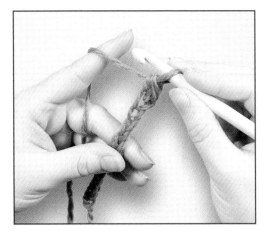

10 To complete a row of single crochet stitches, repeat steps 3 to 9 for each of the following chain stitches in the foundation chain.

Completed row

Row 2

After you work the first row of single crochet stitches into the foundation chain, you can work a new row of single crochet stitches back across the first row. You can continue working rows of single crochet stitches back and forth across your crochet piece to create as many rows as you need.

To start a new row of single crochet stitches, you must first make one chain stitch. This chain stitch is called a *turning chain* and raises the yarn up to the proper height for the new row of single crochet stitches. After you make a turning chain, you must turn your work so that you can crochet back across the previous row.

The chain stitch you make at the beginning of each new row of single crochet stitches is not considered a stitch in the row. When creating rows of single crochet stitches, you do not work into the chain stitch.

To begin the next row of single crochet stitches, you must first make a turning chain to raise the yarn to the required height for the next row. The turning chain for the single crochet stitch is one chain stitch.

1 To make a turning chain, make one chain stitch. To make a chain stitch, see Chapter 2.

2 Turn your work around so that you can crochet back across the previous row.

3 Locate the first single crochet stitch in the previous row. The top of each single crochet stitch has two horizontal strands shaped like a V.

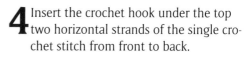

Do not count the base of the turning chain as the first single crochet stitch.

4 Insert the crochet hook under the top two horizontal strands of the single crochet stitch from front to back.

After you complete a row of single crochet stitches, you should count the number of stitches in the row to make sure you have the correct number. Counting stitches will help ensure that you have not worked two stitches into one stitch or skipped a stitch. To count single crochet stitches, place your work on a flat surface and count the vertical part of each stitch, called the *post*. A space separates each stitch in a row.

5 Complete the single crochet stitch.

To complete a single crochet stitch, perform steps 4 to 9 in the instructions for Row 1, sliding the crochet hook through the first two loops in step 6.

6 Repeat steps 4 and 5 for each of the following single crochet stitches in the row.

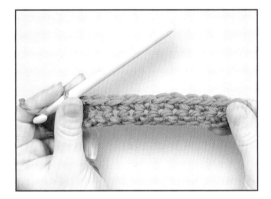

7 To work additional rows of single crochet stitches, repeat steps 1 to 6 for each row you want to complete.

Half Double Crochet

Row 1

The half double crochet stitch is a basic stitch that creates a moderately dense fabric. The half double crochet stitch is slightly taller than the single crochet stitch. In patterns, the half double crochet stitch is abbreviated as **hdc**. A row may be made up entirely of half double crochet stitches or a combination of different stitches.

You work the first row of half double crochet stitches into the foundation chain. The first half double crochet stitch is worked into the third chain stitch. You skip the first two chain stitches in the foundation chain to allow the row of half double crochet stitches to stand at its proper height.

The skipped chain stitches stand up alongside the half double crochet stitches and are considered the first half double crochet stitch in the row.

When locating the third chain stitch, make sure the front of the foundation chain is facing you. The front of the foundation chain displays a row of Vs and is flat. Also, make sure you do not count the loop on the crochet hook as a chain stitch.

1 Make a foundation chain to start your crochet project. To make a foundation chain, see Chapter 2.

2 Locate the third chain stitch from the crochet hook.

3 Bring the yarn over the crochet hook from back to front.

4 Insert the crochet hook under the top loop of the chain stitch, from front to back.

5 Bring the yarn over the crochet hook from back to front.

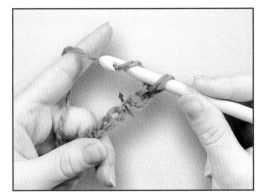

6 Catch the yarn with the hook of the crochet hook.

7 Slide the hook and the strand of yarn through the first loop on the crochet hook, allowing the loop to fall off the crochet hook.

 You now have three loops on the crochet hook.

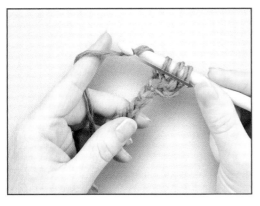

8 Bring the yarn over the crochet hook from back to front.

9 Catch the yarn with the hook of the crochet hook.

10 Slide the hook and the strand of yarn through the three loops on the crochet hook, allowing the three loops to fall off the crochet hook.

When you create the first half double crochet stitch, you skip the first two chain stitches and work into the third chain stitch in the foundation chain. This results in fewer half double crochet stitches than chain stitches. For example, if you have 10 chain stitches in the foundation chain, you will create eight half double crochet stitches in the row. The skipped chain stitches count as one half double crochet stitch, making a total of nine half double crochet stitches in the first row.

 You now have one loop on the crochet hook.

 You have created one half double crochet stitch.

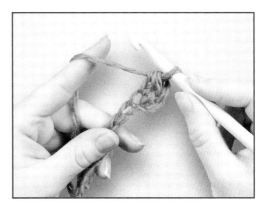

11 To complete a row of half double crochet stitches, repeat steps 3 to 10 for each of the following chain stitches in the foundation chain.

Row 2

To begin the second row of half double crochet stitches, you must first make a turning chain to raise the yarn to the required height for the next row. The turning chain for the half double crochet stitch is two chain stitches. The turning chain counts as the first half double crochet stitch in the row.

1 To make a turning chain, make two chain stitches. To make a chain stitch, see Chapter 2.

2 Turn your work around so that you can crochet back across the previous row.

3 Locate the second half double crochet stitch in the previous row. The top of each half double crochet stitch has two horizontal strands, shaped like a V.

4 Bring the yarn over the crochet hook from back to front.

5 Insert the crochet hook under the top two horizontal strands of the half double crochet stitch from front to back.

Tip ● **Tip** ● **Tip** ● **T**

When working in rows of half double crochet stitches, you can use a safety pin to mark the top chain stitch in a turning chain you make. This will remind you to work a stitch into the turning chain when you reach the turning chain at the end of a row.

6 Complete the half double crochet stitch.

> **Tip**
>
> To complete a half double crochet stitch, perform steps 5 to 10 from the instructions for row 1, sliding the crochet hook through the first two loops in step 7.

7 To complete a row of half double crochet stitches, repeat steps 4 to 6 for each of the remaining half double crochet stitches in the row.

Row 3 and All Remaining Rows

1 To work additional rows of half double crochet stitches, repeat steps 1 to 7 from the row 2 directions for each row you want to complete.

2 When you reach the end of each row, make sure you work a stitch into the top chain stitch of the turning chain in the previous row.

Double Crochet

Row 1

The double crochet stitch is a tall, commonly used stitch that creates a more open fabric than the single crochet stitch.

To work a row of double crochet stitches into the foundation chain, you work the first stitch into the fourth chain stitch. Skipping the first three chain stitches allows the row of double crochet stitches to stand at its proper height. The skipped chain stitches stand up alongside the double crochet stitches and are considered the first double crochet stitch in the row.

When locating the fourth chain stitch in the foundation chain, make sure the front of the foundation chain is facing you. The front of the foundation chain displays a row of Vs and is flat. Also, make sure you do not count the loop on the crochet hook as a chain stitch.

In patterns, the double crochet stitch is abbreviated as **dc**. A row may be made up entirely of double crochet stitches or a combination of different stitches.

1 Make a foundation chain to start your crochet project. To make a foundation chain, see Chapter 2.

2 Locate the fourth chain stitch from the crochet hook.

3 Bring the yarn over the crochet hook from back to front.

4 Insert the crochet hook under the top loop of the chain stitch from front to back.

5 Bring the yarn over the crochet hook from back to front.

6 Catch the yarn with the hook of the crochet hook.

7 Slide the hook and the strand of yarn through the first loop on the crochet hook, allowing the loop to fall off the crochet hook.

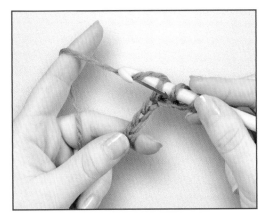

You now have two loops on the crochet hook.

11 Bring the yarn over the crochet hook from back to front.

12 Catch the yarn with the hook of the crochet hook.

13 Slide the hook and the strand of yarn through the two loops, allowing the two loops to fall off the crochet hook.

 You have created one double crochet stitch.

TIP

When you create the first double crochet stitch, you skip the first three chain stitches and work into the fourth chain stitch in the foundation chain. This results in fewer double crochet stitches than chain stitches. For example, if you have 10 chain stitches in the foundation chain, you will create seven double crochet stitches in the row. The skipped chain stitches count as one double crochet stitch, making a total of eight double crochet stitches in the first row.

 You now have three loops on the crochet hook.

8 Bring the yarn over the crochet hook from back to front.

9 Catch the yarn with the hook of the crochet hook.

10 Slide the hook and the strand of yarn through the first two loops on the crochet hook, allowing the two loops to fall off the crochet hook.

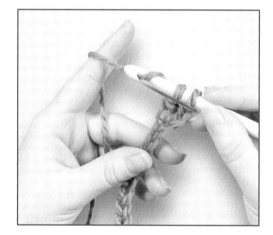

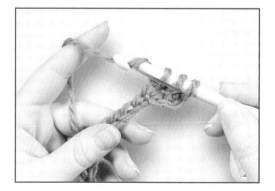

14 To complete a row of double crochet stitches, repeat steps 3 to 13 for each of the following chain stitches in the foundation chain.

After you work the first row of double crochet stitches, you can work a new row of double crochet stitches back across the first row. You can continue working rows of double crochet stitches back and forth across your piece to create as many rows as you need.

To start a new row of double crochet stitches, you must first make three chain stitches. These chain stitches are called a turning chain and raise the yarn up to the proper height for the new row of double crochet stitches. After you make a turning chain, you must turn your work around so that you can crochet back across the previous row.

At the beginning of each new row of double crochet stitches, the turning chain you make is considered the first double crochet stitch in the row. As you crochet rows of double crochet stitches, you work a double crochet stitch into the top chain stitch of each turning chain.

Row 2

To begin the next row of double crochet stitches, you must first make a turning chain to raise the yarn to the required height for the next row. The turning chain for the double crochet stitch is three chain stitches. The turning chain counts as the first double crochet stitch in the row.

1 To make a turning chain, make three chain stitches. To make a chain stitch, see Chapter 2.

2 Turn your work around so that you can crochet back across the previous row.

3 Locate the second double crochet stitch in the previous row. The top of each double crochet stitch has two horizontal strands shaped like a V.

4 Bring the yarn over the crochet hook from back to front.

5 Insert the crochet hook under the top two horizontal strands of the double crochet stitch from front to back.

Row 3 and All Remaining Rows

1 To work additional rows of double crochet stitches, repeat steps 1 to 7 for each row you want to complete.

2 When you reach the end of each row, make sure you work a stitch into the top chain stitch of the turning chain in the previous row.

To correct a mistake, remove the loop from the crochet hook. Then gently pull on the strand of yarn connected to the ball of yarn to unravel your stitches until you reach the first stitch past the mistake. With the front of your crochet piece facing you, re-insert the crochet hook into the front of the loop and begin crocheting again.

6 Complete the double crochet stitch.

To complete a double crochet stitch, perform steps 5 to 13 from the instructions for Row 1, sliding the crochet hook through the first two loops in step 7.

7 To complete a row of double crochet stitches, repeat steps 4 to 6 for each of the remaining double crochet stitches in the row.

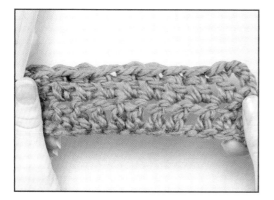

Triple Crochet

Row 1

The triple crochet stitch, also known as the treble crochet stitch, is one of the tallest crochet stitches and creates an airy, delicate fabric. In patterns, the triple crochet stitch is abbreviated as **tr**.

You work the first row of triple crochet stitches into the foundation chain. The first triple crochet stitch is worked into the fifth chain stitch. Skipping the first four chain stitches allows the row of triple crochet stitches to stand at its proper height.

When locating the fifth chain stitch, make sure the front of the foundation chain is facing you and you do not count the loop on the crochet hook as a chain stitch. The front of the foundation chain displays a row of Vs.

After you complete the first row of triple crochet stitches, you should count the stitches in the row to ensure you have the correct number. Make sure you count the skipped chain stitches as one triple crochet stitch. You will have fewer triple crochet stitches than chain stitches in the foundation chain. For example, if you have 10 chain stitches, you will have seven triple crochet stitches.

1 Make a foundation chain to start your crochet project. To make a foundation chain, see Chapter 2.

2 Locate the fifth chain stitch from the crochet hook.

3 Bring the yarn over the crochet hook twice, from back to front.

4 Insert the crochet hook under the top loop of the chain stitch from front to back.

5 Bring the yarn over the crochet hook from back to front.

6 Catch the yarn with the hook of the crochet hook.

7 Slide the hook and the strand of yarn through the first loop on the crochet hook, allowing the loop to fall off the crochet hook.

Tip

One common variation of the triple crochet stitch is the double triple crochet stitch (**dtr**). To make a double triple crochet stitch, perform steps 1 to 11 as shown for triple crochet stitch, locating the sixth chain stitch in step 2 and bringing the yarn over the crochet hook three times in step 3. After you complete the steps, you will have two loops remaining on the crochet hook. Bring the yarn over the crochet hook once again and then slide the hook through the two loops. You have created one double triple crochet stitch. When working in rows of double triple crochet stitches, you will need to make five chain stitches for the turning chain.

�֎ You now have four loops on the crochet hook.

8 Bring the yarn over the crochet hook from back to front.

9 Catch the yarn with the hook of the crochet hook.

10 Slide the hook and the strand of yarn through the first two loops on the crochet hook, allowing the two loops to fall off the crochet hook.

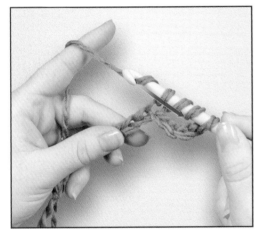

11 Repeat steps 8 to 10 twice to end up with one loop on the crochet hook.

�֎ You now have one loop on the crochet hook.

✖ You have created one triple crochet stitch.

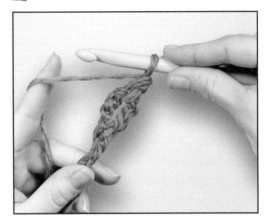

12 To complete a row of triple crochet stitches, repeat steps 3 to 11 for each of the following chain stitches in the foundation chain.

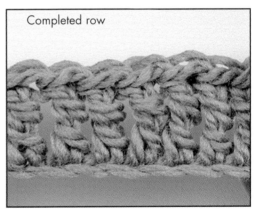

Completed row

After working the first row of triple crochet stitches, you can work the second row of triple crochet stitches back across the first row. You can continue working rows of triple crochet stitches back and forth across the piece to create as many rows as you need.

To start a new row of triple crochet stitches, you must first make four chain stitches. These chain stitches are called a turning chain and raise the yarn up to the proper height for the new row of triple crochet stitches. After you make the turning chain, you must turn your work around so that you can crochet back across the previous row.

At the beginning of each new row of triple crochet stitches, the turning chain you make is considered the first triple crochet stitch in the row. As you crochet rows of triple crochet stitches, you work a triple crochet stitch into the top chain stitch of each turning chain.

To begin the next row of triple crochet stitches, you must first make a turning chain to raise the yarn to the required height for the next row. The turning chain for the triple crochet stitch is four chain stitches. The turning chain counts as the first triple crochet stitch in the row.

Row 2

1 To make a turning chain, make four chain stitches. To make a chain stitch, see Chapter 2.

2 Turn your work around so that you can crochet back across the previous row.

You must make a turning chain at the beginning of each new row of stitches. If you do not make a turning chain, the yarn will not be raised up to accommodate the height of the new row of stitches and the edges of your work will become compressed. For the triple, double, and half double crochet stitches, your rows will also be short a stitch, causing the edges of your work to slope inward. The graphic below shows the height of the basic crochet stitches and the height of the turning chain required by each stitch.

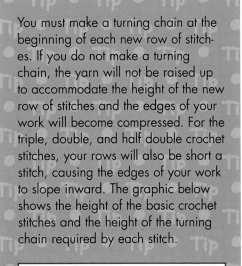

3 Locate the second triple crochet stitch in the previous row. The top of each triple crochet stitch has two horizontal strands, shaped like a V.

4 Bring the yarn over the crochet hook twice, from back to front.

5 Insert the crochet hook under the top two horizontal strands of the triple crochet stitch from front to back.

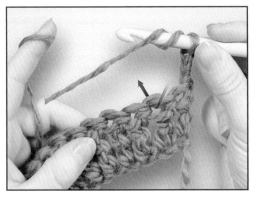

6 Complete the triple crochet stitch.

> **Tip • Tip • Tip • Tip**
>
> To complete a triple crochet stitch, perform steps 5 to 11 from the instructions for Row 1, sliding the crochet hook through the first two loops in step 7.

7 To complete a row of triple crochet stitches, repeat steps 4 to 6 for each of the remaining triple crochet stitches in the row.

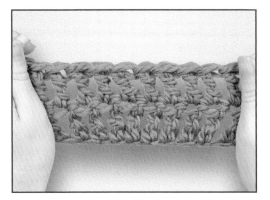

Row 3 and All Remaining Rows

1 To work additional rows of triple crochet stitches, repeat steps 1 to 7 from the Row 2 directions for each row you want to complete.

2 When you reach the end of each row, make sure you work a stitch into the top chain stitch of the turning chain in the previous row.

Make a Slip Stitch

The slip stitch is a versatile stitch that can be used for many purposes. The slip stitch is the shortest crochet stitch and is abbreviated as **sl st** in patterns.

When you have completed a crocheted piece, such as a baby blanket, you can use a row of slip stitches to create a firm edge for the piece. You can also use the slip stitch to carry yarn across the top of existing stitches without adding any noticeable height to your work.

The slip stitch is also used to join crocheted pieces together to assemble your work. When working in rounds to create circular crocheted pieces, you use the slip stitch to join the ends of a round together. For more information on assembling your work and working in rounds, see the "Assemble Your Crocheted Pieces" section later in this chapter.

You can also use the slip stitch to join a new ball of yarn to your crochet project when working in rounds. This is useful if your current ball runs out or you introduce a new color to your project. For information on joining new yarn, see the "Join New Yarn" section later in this chapter.

1 Make one or more rows of a crochet stitch.

Tip

To make one or more rows of a single crochet stitch, see the "Single Crochet" section of this chapter.

2 Turn your work around so that you can crochet back across the previous row.

3 Locate the first crochet stitch from the crochet hook. The top of each crochet stitch has two horizontal strands shaped like a V.

4 Insert the crochet hook under the top two horizontal strands of the crochet stitch from front to back.

7 Slide the hook and the strand of yarn through the three loops on the crochet hook, allowing the three loops to fall off the crochet hook.

 You now have one loop on the crochet hook.

 You have created one slip stitch.

8 To create additional slip stitches, repeat steps 4 to 7 for each of the following crochet stitches in the row.

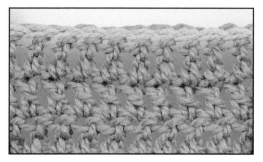

FUN FACT

The slip stitch is not commonly used to create fabric. The slip stitch is a functional stitch that helps you complete tasks such as creating a firm edge, carrying yarn from one place to another, and joining crocheted pieces together.

Unlike other crochet stitches, when starting a new row of slip stitches, you do not have to make a turning chain to raise the yarn for the new row. Slip stitches are the shortest crochet stitch and do not require the height provided by a turning chain.

5 Bring the yarn over the crochet hook from back to front.

6 Catch the yarn with the hook of the crochet hook.

We use a different color of yarn to crochet the slip stitches so that they show up more clearly in this example. You should use the same yarn you used to crochet the piece.

Check Your Gauge

Gauge, or tension, is the number of stitches and rows you produce per inch when crocheting. Gauge determines the size of your finished project.

Before you begin any project, you should always crochet a gauge swatch using the same yarn and crochet hook you will use for the project. A gauge swatch is a piece of crocheted fabric, usually at least a 4-inch square, which allows you to determine if you are producing the correct number of stitches and rows per inch.

Pattern instructions indicate both the number of stitches and the number of rows for the required gauge. For example, a pattern may specify "14 single crochet stitches = 4 inches" and "16 rows = 4 inches" for the gauge.

If you have too many stitches or rows for the required gauge, use a larger crochet hook and try crocheting another gauge swatch. If you have too few stitches or rows, try using a smaller crochet hook. You should not proceed with the project until you have attained the required gauge.

1 Make a foundation chain that measures more than four inches long. To make a foundation chain, see Chapter 2.

2 Create rows of double crochet stitches until your crocheted piece measures more than 4 inches high. To create rows of double crochet stitches, see the "Double Crochet" section of this chapter.

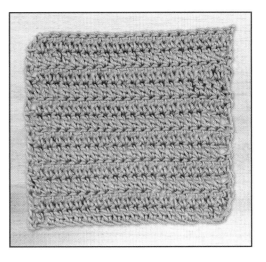

> **Tip**
>
> Your pattern may indicate a different type of stitch or pattern to use for the gauge swatch. In step 2, crochet that stitch or pattern instead.

3 Fasten off the last stitch in the last row. To fasten off, the "Finishing Your Work" section of this chapter.

4 Smooth out the crocheted piece on a flat surface.

5 Place a ruler horizontally on the crocheted piece and mark four inches with pins.

6 Count the number of stitches between the pins.

In addition to the size of the crochet hook, yarn thickness, and type of stitch you are using, gauge can also be affected by how you hold the yarn. Beginners tend to hold the yarn tightly as they crochet; as a result, beginners tend to produce more stitches per inch than they should.

Some patterns may provide the gauge for a gauge swatch that is smaller than a 4-inch square. A smaller gauge swatch, however, is not an adequate sample to accurately measure the gauge. You should convert the gauge given in the pattern to determine the number of stitches and rows for a 4-inch square.

FUN FACT
Gauge swatches are cool gifts for Mom or Dad for all sorts of uses. You can use them as dust cloths or polishing cloths! Even your mistakes are useful for cleaning.

If you do not make a gauge swatch and your project turns out too big or too small, you will be disappointed by the hours of work and cost of materials that have been wasted. Take the time to produce a gauge swatch so that you can be confident your project will turn out the way you expect.

Using a Stitch Gauge

1 Create your gauge swatch by performing steps 1 to 3 in the "Check Your Gauge" section of this chapter.

2 Place a stitch gauge in the center of your crocheted piece.

3 Count the number of stitches and rows within the opening of the stitch gauge.

4 Compare the number of stitches and rows you counted to the numbers given in your pattern.

7 Place a ruler on the crocheted piece vertically and mark 4 inches with pins.

8 Count the number of rows between the pins.

9 Compare the number of stitches and rows you counted to the numbers given in your pattern.

Increase Stitches

Adding stitches to your crochet project is called *increasing*. Increasing stitches widens your fabric and allows you to shape items such as hats and sweaters.

To increase stitches, you can work two or more stitches into one stitch. You can also increase stitches by working two or more stitches into the space between stitches. Increasing stitches by working into a space is commonly done when making a granny square. For information on making a granny square, see the "Crochet Designs" section at the end of this chapter.

Increasing stitches adds stitches to the current row. For example, if you work two stitches into a stitch, you increase the number of stitches in the row by one. If you work three stitches into a stitch, you increase the number of stitches in the row by two. You can increase stitches at the beginning, middle, or end of a row.

1 Crochet to where you want to make an increase.

2 Work a crochet stitch into the next stitch.

You usually work the same type of crochet stitch that is currently in the row, such as a single crochet, half double crochet, double crochet, or triple crochet.

3 Work another crochet stitch of the same type into the same stitch.

❋ You have completed the increase.

The pattern you are using to make your crochet project will specify where to make an increase and the type of stitch to use. For example, a pattern may specify "3 dc in next sp," which means you need to work three double crochet stitches into the next space.

A crochet pattern may indicate an increase using the abbreviation **inc**. For example, "inc 1 sc at each edge" means you need to work two single crochet stitches into the first and the last stitch in the row.

Increase Stitches into a Space

1 Crochet to where you want to make an increase.

2 Work a crochet stitch into the next space.

3 Work two more crochet stitches of the same type into the same space.

❊ You have completed the increase.

Decrease Stitches

You can decrease the number of stitches in your work to make your crochet project narrower. Decreasing stitches allows you to contour your work to create shaped items such as sweaters, socks, and mittens.

To make a decrease, you begin with two partially completed crochet stitches and then combine them to create one stitch. For every decrease you make, you will have one less stitch to work into when you crochet the next row.

You will usually use the method described below to decrease crochet stitches in the second row or the following rows. When decreasing crochet stitches in a row, you can decrease stitches at the beginning, middle, or end of a row.

You can also use the method described below to decrease stitches when working in rounds to create circular crocheted pieces. For information on working in rounds, see the "Work in Rounds" section later in this chapter.

Following are the instructions for decreasing for each of the stitches described in this chapter.

Single Crochet Decrease

1 Crochet to where you want to make a decrease.

2 Work a single crochet stitch into the next stitch until the single crochet stitch is one step from completion. You will have two loops on the crochet hook.

3 Work a single crochet stitch into the next stitch until you have three loops on the crochet hook.

4 Bring the yarn over the crochet hook from back to front.

5 Catch the yarn with the hook of the crochet hook.

6 Slide the hook and the strand of yarn through the three loops on the crochet hook, allowing the three loops to fall off the crochet hook.

❋ You have decreased the number of single crochet stitches by one.

You will see two abbreviations commonly used in patterns to indicate that you should make a single crochet decrease—**sc2tog** and **1 sc dec**. The **sc2tog** abbreviation stands for "single crochet two together." The **1 sc dec** abbreviation stands for "one single crochet decrease."

In pattern instructions, a half double crochet decrease can be represented by the abbreviation **hdc2tog** or the abbreviation **1 hdc dec**. The **hdc2tog** abbreviation stands for "half double crochet two together." The abbreviation **1 hdc dec** stands for "one half double crochet decrease."

Half Double Crochet Decrease

1 Crochet to where you want to make a decrease.

2 Work a half double crochet stitch into the next stitch until the half double crochet stitch is one step from completion. You will have three loops on the crochet hook.

3 Work a half double crochet stitch into the next stitch until you have five loops on the crochet hook.

4 Bring the yarn over the crochet hook from back to front.

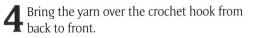

5 Catch the yarn with the hook of the crochet hook.

6 Slide the hook and the strand of yarn through the five loops on the crochet hook, allowing the five loops to fall off the crochet hook.

❋ You have decreased the number of half double crochet stitches by one.

Removing stitches from your work, called *decreasing*, allows you to reduce the width of your crochet project. Removing stitches is useful if you are creating a project, such as a hat, that gradually gets narrower.

To decrease stitches in your work, you merge two partially completed crochet stitches together to form a single stitch. In the next row, you will have one stitch to work into at the location of the decrease, instead of two stitches.

You will usually use the method described below to decrease crochet stitches in the second row or the following rows. When decreasing crochet stitches in a row, you can decrease stitches at the beginning, middle, or end of a row.

You can use the method described below to decrease stitches when working in rounds to create circular crocheted pieces.

Double Crochet Decrease

1 Crochet to where you want to make a decrease.

2 Work a double crochet stitch into the next stitch until the double crochet stitch is one step from completion. You will have two loops on the crochet hook.

3 Work a double crochet stitch into the next stitch until you have three loops on the crochet hook.

4 Bring the yarn over the crochet hook from back to front.

5 Catch the yarn with the hook of the crochet hook.

6 Slide the hook and the strand of yarn through the three loops on the crochet hook, allowing the three loops to fall off the crochet hook.

You have decreased the number of double crochet stitches by one.

Tip

In pattern instructions, a double crochet decrease can be indicated by the abbreviation **dc2tog** (double crochet two together) or the abbreviation **1 dc dec** (one double crochet decrease). A triple crochet decrease can be indicated by the abbreviation **tr2tog** (triple crochet two together) or the abbreviation **1 tr dec** (one triple crochet decrease).

Some patterns may tell you to simply skip over a stitch in a row or round of stitches to make a decrease. When working in rows, you may be instructed not to make a turning chain, which will also reduce the number of stitches in your work. You should always follow the pattern instructions to make your decreases.

Triple Crochet Decrease

1 Crochet to where you want to make a decrease.

2 Work a triple crochet stitch into the next stitch until the triple crochet stitch is one step from completion. You will have two loops on the crochet hook.

3 Work a triple crochet stitch into the next stitch until you have three loops on the crochet hook.

4 Bring the yarn over the crochet hook from back to front.

5 Catch the yarn with the hook of the crochet hook.

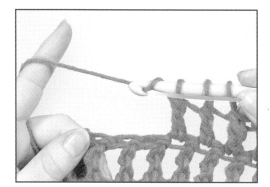

6 Slide the hook and the strand of yarn through the three loops on the crochet hook, allowing the three loops to fall off the crochet hook.

Work in Rounds

You can work in rounds to create flat, circular crocheted pieces, often called *motifs*. When using the method shown below to work in rounds, the first step is to create a foundation chain and join the ends of the foundation chain to make a ring. The ring will form the center of your crocheted piece.

To start each round, you must make a starting chain to raise the yarn up to the proper height for the new round of stitches. The number of chain stitches required for the starting chain depends on the type of crochet stitch that you will work in the round. A round of single crochet requires one chain stitch. A round of half double crochet requires two chain stitches. A round of double crochet requires three chain stitches. A round of triple crochet requires four chain stitches.

After you make the starting chain, you work the first round of crochet stitches by inserting the crochet hook into the center of the ring. You complete the crochet stitches as you would complete crochet stitches when working in rows. When working in rounds, you crochet with the right side of your work always facing you.

Make a Ring

1 Make a foundation chain to start your crochet project.

2 Insert the crochet hook under the top loop of the first chain stitch you made, from front to back.

3 Bring the yarn over the crochet hook from back to front.

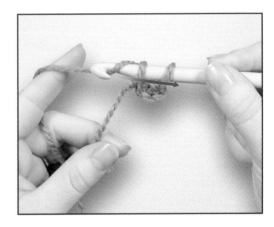

4 Catch the yarn with the hook of the crochet hook.

5 Slide the hook and the strand of yarn through the two loops on the crochet hook, allowing the two loops to fall off the crochet hook.

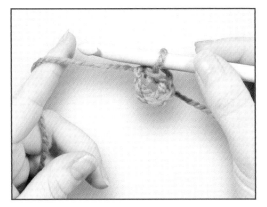

※ You now have one loop on the crochet hook.

※ You have created a slip stitch and made a ring.

FUN FACT
Depending on the pattern you are using, you can work in rounds to create shapes such as hexagons, ovals, and squares. Creating squares, called granny squares, is a common task in crochet.

Round 1

To begin a round of crochet stitches, you must first make a starting chain to raise the yarn to the proper height for the new round.

1 To make a starting chain, make the required number of chain stitches.

Tip

A round of single crochet requires one chain stitch. Half double crochet requires two chain stitches. Double crochet requires three chain stitches. Triple crochet requires four chain stitches.

2 Work a crochet stitch by inserting the crochet hook into the center of the ring from front to back.

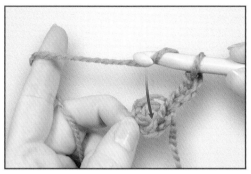

> ● Tip ● Tip ● Tip ● T
> In this example, we complete a double crochet stitch.
> ● Tip ● Tip ● Tip ● T

3 Repeat step 2, rotating the ring clockwise until you have completed all the crochet stitches for the first round.

4 To close the round, insert the crochet hook under the top two horizontal strands of the top chain stitch of the starting chain, from front to back.

5 Bring the yarn over the crochet hook from back to front.

6 Catch the yarn with the hook of the crochet hook.

7 Slide the hook and the strand of yarn through all the loops on the crochet hook, allowing the loops to fall off the crochet hook.

✳ You have created a slip stitch and closed the round.

8 To add a visual reminder of where the round ends and help you keep track of the number of rounds you have completed, you can mark the slip stitch with a stitch marker or safety pin.

Round 2 and Additional Rounds

To start the second and all additional rounds of crochet stitches, you must first make a starting chain as you did for the first round. You work the second round of crochet stitches into the top of the stitches in the previous round. When working in rounds of triple, double, and half double crochet, you work into the second stitch in the previous round. When working in rounds of single crochet, you work into the first stitch in the previous round.

To create a flat piece when working in rounds, you must increase stitches in the second and all subsequent rounds. The example shown below increases stitches by working two stitches into every stitch in the previous round, but you should follow your pattern instructions to determine where to make your increases.

Creating a tube-shaped piece allows you to crochet items such as socks and toys. To make a tube-shaped piece, you do not need to increase stitches in the second and subsequent rounds. Instead, when you crochet the second and subsequent rounds, you can work one stitch into each of the stitches in the previous round. This will create rounds of stitches that stack up one on top of the other, forming a tube-shaped piece.

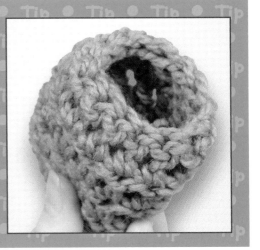

1 To make a starting chain for the new round of stitches, perform step 1 from the Round 1 instructions.

2 Work a crochet stitch under the top two horizontal strands of the second crochet stitch in the previous round.

3 To increase the number of stitches in the round to create a flat piece, work another crochet stitch of the same type into the same crochet stitch.

4 Continue to work two stitches into each of the following crochet stitches in the previous round until you complete all the stitches in the round.

5 To close the round, perform steps 4 to 8 from the Round 1 instructions.

Join New Yarn

You can easily join a new ball of yarn to your project. Joining a new ball of yarn is useful if the ball you are currently using runs out or you want to introduce a new color of yarn to your project.

When working in rows, you join new yarn within a stitch. You can join yarn within any kind of stitch, including single crochet, half double crochet, double crochet, and triple crochet.

You can join new yarn at the beginning, middle, or end of a row. You should try to join new yarn at the end of a row when you find the ball you are currently using is running out. When you need to change colors, you can join new yarn anywhere in a row.

When working in rounds, you use a slip stitch at the end of a round to join new yarn. You usually join new yarn only at the end of a round.

When Working in Rows

1 To join yarn at the end of a row, work the last crochet stitch in the row until the stitch is one step from completion.

> **Tip**
>
> To join yarn within a row, work the stitch before the location where you want to join new yarn until the stitch is one step from completion.

A single, double, or triple crochet stitch will have two loops remaining on the crochet hook. A half double crochet stitch will have three loops remaining on the crochet hook.

2 Catch the new yarn with the hook of the crochet hook, leaving a tail of yarn approximately six inches long.

3 Slide the hook and the new strand of yarn through all the loops on the crochet hook, allowing all the loops to fall off the crochet hook.

4 Cut the old yarn, leaving a tail of yarn approximately six inches long.

When you finish your project, you can weave in the yarn ends. For information on weaving in yarn ends, see the "Finishing Your Work" section of this chapter.

5 Continue crocheting with the new yarn.

Tip ● Tip ● Tip ● Ti

To weave in yarn ends as you work, lay the new yarn on top of the stitches in the previous row a few inches before you want to use the new yarn. Crochet across the row as you normally would. When you reach the location where you want to use the new yarn, perform steps 1 to 4 to secure the new yarn. Lay the tail of the old yarn on top of the stitches in the previous row and crochet across the row with the new yarn for a few inches. Then cut the tail of the old yarn close to the surface of your work.

Tip ● Tip ● Tip ● Ti

When Working in Rounds

1 Work the last crochet stitch in the round.

2 Insert the crochet hook under the top two horizontal strands of the top chain stitch in the starting chain from front to back.

3 Catch the new yarn with the hook of the crochet hook, leaving a tail of yarn approximately six inches long.

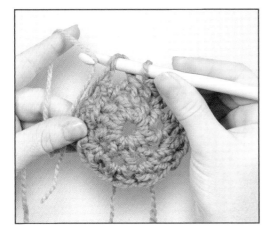

4 Slide the hook and the new strand of yarn through all the loops on the crochet hook, allowing all the loops to fall off the crochet hook.

You have created a slip stitch and joined the new yarn.

5 Cut the old yarn, leaving a tail of yarn approximately six inches long.

6 Continue crocheting with the new yarn.

When you finish your project, you can weave in the yarn ends. For information on weaving in yarn ends, see the following "Finishing Your Work" section.

Finishing Your Work

Proper finishing techniques can help you create a professional-looking crocheted piece. In this section you will learn how to fasten off the last stitch of your crocheted piece and then how to conceal all the dangling yarn ends that were left when you started a new ball of yarn and when you fastened off your last stitch.

Fasten Off

After you complete the last crochet stitch in your work, one loop will remain on your crochet hook. You must *fasten off* this loop to prevent your work from unraveling when you remove the crochet hook. When fastening off, leave a six inch tail of yarn that will be woven into the crocheted piece later.

1 Complete the last crochet stitch in the last row. You should have one loop on the crochet hook.

2 Cut the strand of yarn connected to the ball, leaving a tail of yarn approximately six inches long.

If you plan to use the tail of yarn to sew pieces of your work together, leave a longer tail. For information on sewing your work together, see the "Assemble Your Crocheted Pieces" section.

3 Bring the yarn over the crochet hook from back to front.

4 Catch the yarn with the hook of the crochet hook.

5 Slide the hook and the strand of yarn through the loop on the crochet hook, pulling the entire strand of yarn through the loop.

6 Pull the yarn gently to tighten.

Weave In Yarn Ends

Once you finish a project, you need to conceal all the dangling ends of yarn left over from creating the foundation chain, fastening off, and from where you started new balls of yarn. Weaving in yarn ends allows you to incorporate the loose ends of yarn seamlessly into your crocheted fabric.

You weave in yarn ends on the wrong side of your work to keep the right side smooth and neat. To weave in a yarn end securely, you weave the yarn end two inches in one direction and then back an inch in the opposite direction.

1 Thread a yarn end through a tapestry needle.

2 With the wrong side of your work facing you, insert the tapestry needle into the stitches across your crocheted piece for approximately two inches.

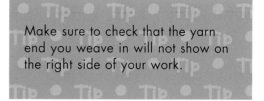

Make sure to check that the yarn end you weave in will not show on the right side of your work.

3 Reverse the direction of the tapestry needle, skip a crochet stitch, and then insert the needle back into the same stitches across your crocheted piece for approximately one inch.

4 Cut the end of the yarn close to the surface of your work.

5 Gently stretch your work in each direction to pull the yarn end into the work.

6 Repeat steps 1 to 5 for each yarn end you want to weave into your work.

Assemble Your Crocheted Pieces

Using the Invisible Seam

When all the pieces of your crochet project are complete, you can join, or *seam*, the pieces together. There are three commonly used seams for joining crocheted pieces—invisible seam, overcast seam, and slip stitch seam. The invisible seam, also called the mattress stitch seam, produces a flat, smooth, flexible seam that is almost undetectable. This seam is ideal for assembling garments, particularly baby clothes.

In the example below, we use the invisible seam to join the side edges of crocheted pieces. You can also use this seam to join the top edges of crocheted pieces.

To use the invisible seam to join side edges, your crocheted pieces should have the same number of rows and the rows should be aligned before you start. You can use straight pins to hold the crocheted pieces in place as you sew. When sewing the invisible seam, the right side of your work faces you, allowing you to see how the seam will look when finished.

1 Place the two crocheted pieces you want to sew together side by side with the right sides facing you, the bottom edges at the bottom, and the rows lined up.

2 Cut a strand of yarn long enough to sew the crocheted pieces together.

3 Thread the strand of yarn through a tapestry needle, leaving a tail approximately six inches long.

We use a different color of yarn to sew the crocheted pieces together to more clearly show the example. You should use the same yarn you used to crochet the pieces.

4 On the bottom right corner of the left crocheted piece, from the back of the piece, insert the needle through the bottom of the first stitch. Then pull the yarn through.

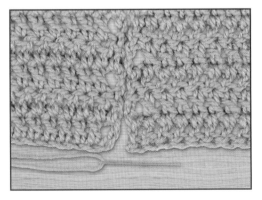

5 On the bottom left corner of the right crocheted piece, from the front of the piece, insert the needle through the bottom of the first stitch. Then pull the yarn through.

Some crochet patterns may instruct you to block your crocheted pieces before you assemble them. Blocking involves dampening the pieces so that you can shape the pieces to their proper dimensions and flatten curling edges. In most cases, however, you will find that your pieces require little or no blocking, since crocheting usually produces a firm fabric that retains its shape.

6 On the bottom right corner of the left crocheted piece, from the back of the piece, insert the needle through the bottom of the first stitch again. Then pull the yarn through to secure the yarn.

7 On the first row of the right crocheted piece, insert the needle up through the first stitch, catching one or two loops of the stitch. Then pull the yarn through.

8 On the first row of the left crocheted piece, insert the needle up through the first stitch, catching one or two loops of the stitch. Then pull the yarn through.

9 Repeat steps 7 and 8, moving up one row at a time on each crocheted piece, until you have sewed the entire edge.

Using the Overcast Seam

You can use the overcast seam, also called the whip stitch seam, to sew your crocheted pieces together. This seam can be used to assemble the pieces of a garment.

The overcast seam is usually worked with the right sides of your crocheted pieces facing each other and the edges lined up. You can pin the pieces together to make sure they do not move while you sew the seam. You sew the overcast seam from right to left, using a strand of the same yarn you used to crochet the pieces. Be careful not to sew the overcast seam too tightly. After you complete the seam, there will be ends of yarn hanging from your project. You can later weave the yarn ends into your project.

In the example below, we use the overcast seam to join the top edges of crocheted pieces. You can also use the overcast seam to join the side edges of crocheted pieces.

1 Cut a strand of yarn long enough to sew the crocheted pieces together.

2 Thread the strand of yarn through a tapestry needle, leaving a tail approximately six inches long.

> **Tip**
>
> We use a different color of yarn to sew the crocheted pieces together to more clearly show the example. You should use the same yarn you used to crochet the pieces.

3 Hold the two crocheted pieces you want to sew together with the right sides facing each other and the edges lined up. Make sure the edges you want to sew together are at the top.

4 At the top right corner of the crocheted pieces, insert the needle under the top two horizontal strands of the first stitch of both pieces from back to front. Then pull the yarn through.

To create a flatter, smoother overcast seam, perform the steps shown here, except insert the needle through only the outside horizontal strands of the stitches in step 4, instead of all the horizontal strands. This technique is useful when you are using the overcast seam to join granny squares.

5 Bring the needle and yarn over the top edges of the crocheted pieces toward the back of your work.

6 Repeat steps 4 and 5, moving one stitch to the left each time, until you have sewed the entire edge.

Using the Slip Stitch Seam

You can use the slip stitch seam to join your crocheted pieces. The slip stitch creates a strong, inflexible seam that is best suited for joining straight edges, such as the edges of granny squares. The slip stitch seam is not suitable for assembling garments.

You use a crochet hook to make a slip stitch seam. Be careful not to work the slip stitch seam too tightly. To ensure your slip stitch seam is not too tight, you should use the same size hook you used for the crochet project or a hook one size larger. Instead of using a new strand of yarn, you will usually use a tail of yarn from one of the crocheted pieces to seam the pieces together.

In the following example, we crochet the slip stitch seam with the right sides of the pieces together and insert the crochet hook through only the inside horizontal strands of the stitches to make the seam less bulky and less visible.

1 Hold the two crocheted pieces you want to slip stitch together with the right sides facing each other and the edges lined up. Make sure the edges you want to slip stitch together are at the top.

2 At the top right corner of the crocheted pieces, insert the crochet hook under the inside horizontal strands of the first stitch of both pieces, from front to back.

We use a different color of yarn to slip stitch the crocheted pieces together to more clearly show the example. You should use a tail of yarn from one of the crocheted pieces.

3 Bring the tail of yarn you will use to slip stitch the seam over the crochet hook from back to front.

4 Catch the yarn with the hook of the crochet hook.

> **Tip**
>
> You can work the slip stitch on the right side of your project to create a more visible, raised seam, which can add a decorative element to your project. Perform the steps shown here, except hold the wrong sides of your crocheted pieces together in step 1. In step 2, insert the crochet hook under the top two horizontal strands of the first stitch of both pieces, instead of only the inside horizontal strands.

5 Slide the hook and the strand of yarn through all the loops on the crochet hook, allowing all the loops to fall off the crochet hook.

✳ You will have one loop on the crochet hook.

6 Repeat steps 2 to 5, moving one stitch to the left each time, until you have slip stitched the entire edge.

7 When you have slip stitched the entire edge, fasten off the last loop on the crochet hook.

Crochet Designs

Solid Shell Stitch

Abbreviation:

tch = turning chain.

sc = single crochet

ch = chain

dc = double crochet

rep = repeat

Ch 20 for the foundation chain.

Row 1:

1 sc into 2nd ch from hook, *skip 2 chs, 5 dc into next ch, skip 2 chs, 1 sc into next ch; rep from * to end of row, turn.

Row 2:

Ch 3 (counts as 1 dc), 2 dc into first st, *skip 2 dc, 1 sc into next dc, skip 2 dc, 5 dc into next sc; rep from * to end of row, ending last rep with 3 dc into last sc, skip tch, turn.

Row 3:

Ch 1, 1 sc into first st, *skip 2 dc, 5 dc into next sc, skip 2 dc, 1 sc into next dc; rep from * to end of row, ending last rep with 1 sc into top of tch, turn.

Rep Rows 2 and 3.

Griddle Stitch

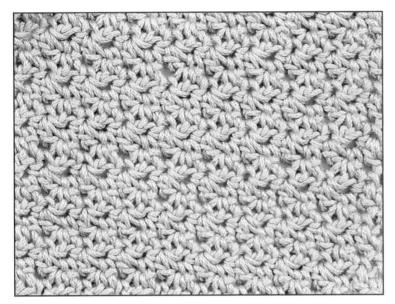

Abbreviation:

tch = turning chain.

sc = single crochet

ch = chain

dc = double crochet

rep = repeat

Ch 22 for the foundation chain.

Row 1:

Skip first 3 chs (counts as 1 dc), *1 sc into next ch, 1 dc into next ch; rep from * to end of row, ending last rep with 1 sc into last ch, turn.

Row 2:

Ch 3 (counts as 1 dc), skip 1 st, *1 sc into next dc, 1 dc into next sc; rep from * to end of row, ending last rep with 1 sc into top of tch, turn.

Rep Row 2.

Granny Square

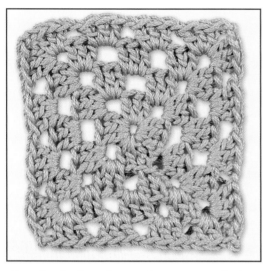

Abbreviation:

tch = turning chain.

sc = single crochet

ch = chain

dc = double crochet

rep = repeat

Ch 5 for the foundation chain. Join with sl st in first ch made to form a ring.

Rnd 1:

Ch 3 (counts as 1 dc), 2 dc into ring. (Ch 2, 3 dc into ring) 3 times. Ch 2. Join with sl st to top of beg ch 3.

Rnd 2:

Sl st into each of next 2 dc and sl st into ch 2 sp of previous row. Ch 3. (2 dc, ch 2, 3 dc) into same space (corner made). *Ch 1, skip next 3 dc and into next ch 2 corner sp work (3 dc, ch 2, 3 dc) (corner made); rep from * twice. Ch 1, skip next 3 dc and join with sl st to top of ch 3.

Rnd 3:

Sl st into each of next 2 dc and sl st into ch 2 sp of previous row. Ch 3. (2 dc, ch 2, 3 dc) into same space (corner made). *Ch 1, skip next 3 dc, 3 dc into next ch 1 sp. Ch 1, skip next 3   dc and into next ch 2 corner sp work (3 dc, ch 2, 3 dc) (corner   made); rep from * twice. Ch 1, 3 dc into next ch 1 sp. Ch 1, skip next 3 dc and join with sl st to top of ch 3.

Rnd 4:

Sl st into each of next 2 dc and sl st into ch 2 sp of previous row. Ch 3. (2 dc, ch 2, 3 dc) into same space (corner made). *(Ch 1, skip next 3 dc, 3 dc into next ch 1 sp) twice. Ch 1, skip next 3 dc and into next corner sp work (3 dc, ch 2, 3 dc); rep from * twice. (Ch 1, skip next 3 dc, 3 dc into next ch 1 sp) twice. Ch 1, skip next 3 dc and join with sl st to top of ch 3.

Chevron Stitch

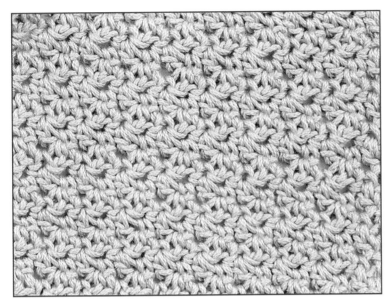

Abbreviation: dc3tog=*yo, insert hook, yo and draw through loop, yo draw through 2 loops *; rep from * to * for next 2 sts to get 4 loops on hook, ending yo, draw through all loops on hook.

tch = turning chain.

Ch 23 for the foundation chain.

Row 1:

Skip 2 chs (counts as 1 dc), 1 dc into next ch, *1 dc into each of the next 3 chs, work dc3tog over the next 3 chs, 1 dc into each of the next 3 chs, 3 dc into next ch; rep from * to end of row, ending last rep with 2 dc into last ch, turn.

Row 2:

Ch 3 (counts as 1 dc), 1 dc into first st, *1 dc into each of the next 3 dc, work dc3tog over the next 3 chs, 1 dc into each of the next 3 dc, 3 dc into next dc; rep from * to end of row, ending last rep with 2 dc into top of tch, turn.

Rep Row 2.

PART 2

You've studied the many types of yarns available. You've shopped, or maybe searched through your Aunt's crochet basket, and you've got some yarn and a crochet hook. You've practiced a few simple stitches. Now it's time to get busy making something fun!

So...let's get started!

The Projects

Project 1
Friendship Bracelets

Project 4
Cute and Comfy Hat

Project 2
Bookmark for Book Worms

Project 5
Shimmering Scarf

Project 3
Little Pink Purse

Project 6
Moonlit Sky Scarf

Friendship Bracelets

Make several of these fun little fashion statements. Wear them on your wrist or ankle. Make one in every color to match all your outfits. Have a friendship bracelet party and make them with your friends.

Materials

Lily Sugar N' Cream (85 gr/150 yds; 100% cotton) remnant

Crochet Hook

Size 4.5mm (US 7) crochet hook

Instructions

1. Ch 20 (or length you wish to fit wrist or ankle).
2. Fasten off. (See page 74.)
3. Thread ends through first ch and tie.

Jennifer Burrell Photography

Bookmark for Book Worms

These handy bookmarks can be made with almost any yarn. They make great gifts for birthdays or holidays. Have a crochet party and make a bunch for a fund raising project.

Materials

Lily Sugar N' Cream (85 gr/150 yds; 100% cotton) 1 ball

Crochet Hook

Size 4.5mm (US 7) crochet hook (or size needed to achieve gauge)

Gauge

14 sc and 15 rows = 4"/10 cm

Instructions

1. Ch 19.
2. **Row 1:** Sc in 2nd ch from hook and every ch along. Turn. Ch 1.
3. Repeat Row 1 13 more times. Fasten off.

Fringe

1. Cut lengths of yarn 12" [30.5 cm] long.
2. Knot into fringe along lower edge by folding yarn in half and pulling loop though edge from back to front with hook.
3. Thread ends through loop and pull to secure.
4. Trim evenly.

Little Pink Purse

When people tell you how cute this little purse is, you can say, "Oh, I made it myself." You are an artist with a crochet hook now!

Materials

Patons SWS (80 gr/110 yds; 70% wool/30% soy)
(#70530 Natural Geranium) 5 balls
One button in a complementary color

Crochet Hook

Size 5.5mm (US 9) crochet hook or size required to achieve gauge

Gauge

14 sts and 6 rows = 4" (10 cm) in dc

Instructions

Back

1. **Ch 30.
2. **Foundation Row:** (RS) 1 dc in 4th ch from hook. 1 dc in each ch to end of ch. 28 dc. Ch 3. Turn.
3. **Row 1:** Miss first dc. 1dc in each dc to end of row. Ch 3. Turn.
4. Rep this Row 1 until work from beginning measures 8.5"/21.5 cm.**
5. Work another 4 rows for flap. Fasten off.

Front

Work from ** to ** as given for back.

Assembly and Strap

1. With WS facing tog and aligning bottom edge, join tog by working 1 row of sc through both thicknesses, from top edge around to other top edge and working an extra 3 sc to ease around corners. Work sc around edge of flap, working an extra 3 sc to ease around corner, to center of flap. Ch 7 (button loop). Join with ss to last sc worked. Cont working sc around rest of flap, working an extra 3 sc to ease around corner.
2. Make a chain 40"/101.5 cm long. Join to other top edge corner and sc in each ch along chain. Fasten off. Sew button to correspond to button loop.

Jennifer Burrell Photography

Cute and Comfy Hat

Keep your ears warm all winter with this cute and comfy little hat. Make it in colors to match your coat. These hats make great Christmas gifts too. A gift you made yourself says "I took the time to make something special just for you."

Materials

Manos del Uruguay wool (100 gr/138 yds; 100% Manos wool) Sage (#107) 1 hank

Crochet Hook

Size 5.5mm (US 9) crochet hook or size required to achieve gauge.

Gauge

16 sts and 24 rows = 4" (10 cm)

Size

One size: 20–21"

Instructions

1. Ch 4. Join with SS to first ch to form ring.

2. **Rnd 1:** Ch 3 (acts as first dc) 8 dc in center of ring. 9 dc. Join with ss to top of ch 3.

3. **Rnd 2:** Ch 3. 1 dc in same sp as last ss. 2dc in each dc around. 18 dc. Join with ss to top of ch 3.

4. **Rnd 3:** Ch 3. 1 dc in same sp as last ss. *1 dc in next dc. 2 dc in next dc. Rep from * around to last dc. 1 dc in last dc. 27 dc. Join with ss to top of ch 3.

5. **Rnd 4:** Ch 3. 1 dc in same sp as last ss. *1 dc in each of the next 2 dc. 2 dc in next dc. Rep from * around to last 2 dc. 1 dc in each of the last 2 dc. 36 dc. Join with ss to top of ch 3.

6. **Rnd 5:** Ch 3. 1 dc in same sp as last ss. *1 dc in each of the next 3 dc. 2 dc in next dc. Rep from * around to last 3 dc. 1 dc in each of the last 3 dc. 45 dc. Join with ss to top of ch 3.

7. **Rnd 6:** Ch 3. 1 dc in same sp as last ss. *1 dc in each of the next 4 dc. 2 dc in next dc. Rep from * around to last 4 dc. 1 dc in each of the last 4 dc. 54 dc. Join with ss to top of ch 3.

8. **Rnd 7:** Ch 3. Miss the first dc (where last ss was worked). 1 dc in next dc and each dc around. Join with ss to top of ch 3.

9. **Rnds 8-15:** As Rnd 7.

10. Fasten off. (See page 74.)

PROJECT 5

Jennifer Burrell Photography

Shimmering Scarf

Make this scarf as a special gift for your best friend. Or just make one to match your best coat and gloves. It's a special, shimmery, soft delight to help you stay warm on chilly winter days.

Materials

Needful Yarns Filtes King Lamé (1.75oz/50g)
MC (Main Color) = #42 Charcoal, 2 balls
Contrast A = #41 Grey, 2 balls

Crochet Hook

Size G/6 US (4.25mm) crochet hook or size needed to obtain gauge

Gauge

18 double crochet and 11 rows = 4" (10cm).

Size

Approximately 60 × 6.75" (152 x 16.5cm)

Instructions

Scarf

1. Beginning at side edge, with MC, ch 270.
2. *Working in dc, work 2 rows in MC, 2 rows in Contrast color.
3. Rep from * 3 times. Work 2 more rows in MC.
4. Fasten off. (See page 74.)
5. Weave in yarn ends. (See page 75.)

> **Abbreviations:**
> ch = chain   dc = double crochet
>
> When working in rows of dc, remember to ch 3 at the end of each row for the turning chain and skip the first dc in the next row. Also, remember to work into the top ch of the previous row's turning chain when you come to it.

Fringe

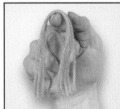   

1. Cut 5 11-inch (28cm) lengths of yarn. Fold the lengths in half.
2. With the right side of the scarf facing you, insert the crochet hook at the edge of your scarf from back to front.
3. With the crochet hook, catch the strands of yarn at the fold.
4. Use the crochet hook to slide the strands of yarn through the scarf. The yarn forms a loop on one side of the scarf.
5. Remove the crochet hook from the yarn.
6. With your fingers, bring the ends of the yarn through the loop.
7. Pull the ends of the yarn to secure the fringe to the scarf.
8. Straighten and trim the fringe.
9. Repeat steps 1 to 8, adding 1 section of fringe to each corresponding row color.

PROJECT **6**

Moonlit Sky Scarf

Here's a more casual scarf. Easy to make and fun to wear for all your winter activities.

Materials

Needful Yarns Ker 1.75oz/50g, #712 Blue, 4 balls

Crochet Hook

Size K/10.5 US (6.5mm) crochet hook or size needed to obtain gauge

Gauge

11 single crochet (sc) and 12 rows = 4" (10cm)

Size

Approximately 80 × 7" (203 x 18cm)

Instructions

Scarf

1. Beginning at side edge, ch 27.
2. **Row 1:** (RS): 1 sc in 6th ch from hook *ch 5.
3. Skip 3 chs. 1 sc into next ch.
4. Rep from * to end of row, turn.
5. **Row 2:** *Ch 5. 1 sc into next 5 ch arch.
6. Rep from * to end of row; turn.
7. Rep Row 2 until work from beginning measures 80 ins (203cm).
8. Fasten off. Weave in yarn ends. (See pages 74–75.)

Fringe

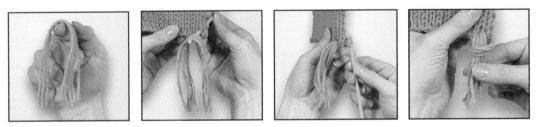

1. Cut 2 lengths of yarn 11 ins (28cm). Fold the lengths in half.
2. With the right side of the scarf facing you, insert the crochet hook at the edge of your scarf from back to front.
3. With the crochet hook, catch the strands of yarn at the fold.
4. Use the crochet hook to slide the strands of yarn through the scarf. The yarn forms a loop on one side of the scarf.
5. Remove the crochet hook from the yarn.
6. With your fingers, bring the ends of the yarn through the loop.
7. Pull the ends of the yarn to secure the fringe to the scarf.
8. Straighten and trim the fringe.
9. Repeat steps 1 to 8, adding 1 section of fringe to each arch.

Jennifer Burrell Photography

Here you will find a glossary of crochet terms and a list of abbreviations used in knitting and crocheting patterns and instructions.

Quick Reference Guide

Glossary

B

Back loop
Of the two horizontal loops of a crochet stitch, the one that is farthest away from you when you are working on a piece.

Backstitch
A strong seaming stitch that is used to sew pieces together.

Blocking
A procedure involving dampening and then shaping a piece to help even out stitches, flatten curling edges, and ensure the piece has the correct dimensions.

Bobbins
Plastic devices that you can use to hold short lengths of yarn when working with multiple yarn colors. Using bobbins helps to prevent tangles.

Button band
A strip of knitted or crocheted fabric onto which you sew buttons.

Buttonhole band
A strip of knitted or crocheted fabric into which you work buttonholes.

C

Chain
A sequence of chain stitches.

Chain stitch
The most basic crochet stitch.

Crochet
To join loops of yarn with a crochet hook to create fabric.

D

Double crochet stitch
A commonly used crochet stitch that creates an open fabric.

Dye lot number
Yarn is dyed in specific lots and each lot is assigned a dye lot number. Balls of yarn that have the same dye lot number will be the same shade.

E

Eyelet
A small, decorative hole. Also a type of lace fabric that features decorative holes.

F

Fasten off
A method of securing the last loop on your crochet hook to prevent your work from unraveling.

Foundation chain
The first row of chain stitches you complete, which forms the base on which you will crochet all the other rows in your piece.

Front loop
Of the two horizontal loops of a crochet stitch, the one that is closest to you when you are working on a piece.

G

Gauge
The number of stitches and rows you should have in a square of knitted or crocheted fabric to ensure your finished project will be the correct size. Also called *tension*.

Gauge swatch
A piece of knitted or crocheted fabric that allows you to determine if you are producing the correct number of stitches and rows per inch for a project.

H

Half double crochet stitch
A basic crochet stitch that creates a moderately dense fabric.

Hank
A loosely twisted coil of yarn. You must wind hanks into balls before working with the yarn.

P

Pattern
A set of instructions for creating a crocheted project.

Post
The vertical part of a crochet stitch. Also called the *leg* or *bar*.

R

Right side
The side of your fabric that will show outside when your project is complete.

S

Seaming
Sewing your finished crocheted pieces together to complete your project. Also called *sewing seams*.

Single crochet stitch
One of the most basic crochet stitches. It is a short stitch that creates a dense fabric.

Skein
An oblong-shaped ball of yarn.

Slip knot
A knot that makes a loop you can use as the starting point for your crochet or knitting project. In knitting, the slip knot serves as your first stitch. In crochet, the slip knot is not counted as a stitch.

Slip stitch
The shortest stitch that can be used to join seams, create firm edges, or carry yarn across stitches.

Stitch
One of a series of loops that hold together to form a piece of fabric. One horizontal line of stitches is called a *row* of stitches.

T

Tail
A strand of yarn that is left over when you begin a piece, finish a piece, or start a new ball of yarn.

Triple crochet stitch
One of the tallest crochet stitches. The triple crochet stitch creates an airy, delicate fabric. Also known as the *treble crochet stitch*.

Turning chain
One or more chain stitches that you make at the beginning of each row of crochet stitches to bring the yarn up to the proper height for the new row.

W

Weaving
A method of securing yarn that is being carried across four or more stitches so that you can make a color change. Also refers to working in a strand of yarn that is left over when you add stitches, finish stitches, or start a new ball of yarn.

Wrong side
The part of a fabric that will face inside when your project is complete.

Y

Yarn end
See tail.

Yarn over
The basic movement used to create stitches.

Yarn winder
A device you can use to wind yarn into balls or skeins.

Common Abbreviations

Alt	alternate or alternating	inc	increase
Approx	approximately	incl	including
Beg	beginning	keep cont	keeping continuity
Bet	between	LH	left hand
bk lp	back loop	Lp	loop
blo	back loop only	LT	left twist
Bp	back post	M	meter
bo	bobble	MC	main color
CC	contrast color	Mm	millimeter
ch(s)	chain stitch(es)	Oz	ounce
cl	cluster	Pat	pattern
CL	cross stitches to the left	Pu	pick up
Cm	centimeter	Rem	remaining
Col	color	Rep	repeat
Cont	continue	RH	right hand
CR	cross stitches to the right	RS	right side
Dc	double crochet	RT	right twist
dc dec	double crochet decrease	Sc	single crochet
dc2tog	double crochet two stitches together	sc dec	single crochet decrease
dec	decrease	sc2tog	single crochet two stitches together
dtr	double triple crochet	sp(s)	space(s)
ea	each	st(s)	stitch(es)
est	established	tch	turning chain
flo	front loop only	tbl	through back loop
foll	follow or following	tog	together
fp	front post	tr	triple crochet or treble crochet
ft	lpfront loop	tr dec	triple crochet decrease
g	gram	tr2tog	triple crochet two stitches together
hdc	half double crochet	WS	wrong side
hdc dec	half double crochet decrease	Wyib	with yarn in back
hdc2tog	half double crochet two stitches together	Wyif	with yarn in front
hk	hook	yb	yarn back or yarn behind
in(s)	inch(es)	yf	yarn forward
		yo	yarn over

INDEX